D1882805

FAITHS, FAIRS AND FESTIVALS OF INDIA

FAITHS, FAIRS
AND
FESTIVALS OF INDIA

C. H. BUCK

GYAN

Published by

GYAN

Gyan Publishing House
5, Ansari Road
Daryaganj, New Delhi-110002
Phone: 011-47034999, 9811692060
E-mail: books@gyanbooks.com

Distribution Network
gyanbooks.com
India, USA, Canada, UK, Australia, France

© Publisher
All rights reserved. No part of this work may be reproduced, stored, adapted, or transmitted in any form or by any means, electronic, mechanical, photocopying, micro-filming, recording or otherwise, or translated in any language, without the prior written permission of the copyright owner and the publisher.

ISBN : 978-81-212-3377-4 (PB)
First Published, Calcutta, 1917

2nd Impression 2020

Printed at: Gyan Press, Delhi.

The book is sold subject to the condition that it shall not, by way of trade or otherwise, be lent, resold, hired out, or otherwise circulated without the prior publisher's written consent.

Faiths, Fairs and Festivals of India
Author: C. H. Buck

FAITHS, FAIRS, AND FESTIVALS OF INDIA

BY

MAJOR C. H. BUCK., I. A.
PUNJAB COMMISSION.

CALCUTTA
THACKER, SPINK & CO
1917

Dedicated

TO

THE MEMORY OF MY UNCLE

SIR EDWARD CHARLES BUCK

Kt., LL.D., K.C.S.I.,

who devoted his life for the benefit of
others and especially for that
of the people of India.

PREFACE.

In this little volume I have attempted to bring together the leading features of the principal Indian religions, to describe some of the chief ceremonies and festivals, and, in the last chapter, to give a few notes on the management of a large religious fair.

I do not profess to have written much which is original, and this little book may be regarded as a simple summary composed from the works of many learned authors.

I trust that my effort will provide a useful work of reference and enable some of my fellow-countrymen, who have not time or inclination to study what is regarded, by many perhaps, as a dry and complex subject, to gain a slight idea of the religious views held by millions of British subjects in India and thus to sympathize with and comprehend them better.

C. H. B.

CONTENTS.

WORKS OF REFERENCE.

Brief History of the Indian Peoples, by W. W. HUNTER.
Census and Settlement Reports.
Cyclopædia of India, by EDWARD BALFOUR.
Early History of India, by VINCENT SMITH.
Encyclopædia Britannica.
Hinduism, Past and Present, by J. MURRAY MITCHELL.
Imperial and District Gazetteers.
Indian Wisdom, by MONIER WILLIAMS.
Islam, by SYED AMEER ALI.
Mystics, Ascetics, and Saints of India, by J. C. OMAN.
Orissa, by W. W. HUNTER.
Parsi, Jaina, and Sikh, by D. M. THORNTON.
Religious Thought and Life in India, by MONIER WILLIAMS.
Sleeman's Rambles.
Studies of Non-Christian Religions, by ELIOT HOWARD.
The Highlands of Central India, by CAPTAIN FORSYTH.
The Holy Qoran, with commentary, by MUHAMMAD ABDUL HAKIM KHAN.
The Koran, with notes, by G. SALE.
The Times of India Illustrated Weekly.
The Twelve Upanishads, by TOOKARAM TATYA.
The West in the East, by PRICE-COLLIER.
The World's Religions, by G. T. BETTANY.
Tod's Rajasthan, annotated, by VINCENT SMITH.
Useful Tables, by PRINSEP.
Western Tibet, by CH. A. SHERRING.

FAITHS, FAIRS, AND FESTIVALS OF INDIA.

CHAPTER I.

INTRODUCTION.

IN order to perceive how the religions of India have taken shape, it is convenient to trace briefly the history of the principal races which have peopled the country.

We must go back to the aboriginal or primitive tribes, about whose origin so little is known positively. Some of them are believed to have entered India at various times, several thousands of years before Christ, from the neighbourhood of Tartary and Tibet. Next we have the Kolarians, who apparently came from the same direction and, passing through Bengal, finally settled in the mountainous regions of the central portion of India. Thirdly there are the great Dravidian races in Southern India, whose antecedents seem to have advanced into the country through the passes of the north-west.

These were the three main stocks of primitive tribes first known to have occupied the Peninsula; most of them were of small stature and dark skin, with flat noses and low foreheads.

The Gonds and Korkus in Central India, the Bhils in the hills to the west, the Kondhs in Gondvana and Orissa, the Santhals and Kols in the hilly tracts north of the Ganges in Bengal, the Khasias and Garos on the eastern border, the Puliyars and Nairs of the Madras hills, the savages of the Andaman Islands, and the celebrated Gurkhas in the neighbourhood of Nepal are representatives of these ancient races.

Some two thousand years before Christ there came about a great upheaval in Central Asia in the region which surrounds the sources of the Oxus; members of a great primeval race, who called themselves Arya, spread abroad into Europe, Persia, and India. They were a people of good physique, with fair complexions and fine features; the skin of those who resided in the plains of India became darkened, while that of the others who dwelt in the cooler climes of Europe assumed a paler hue. Their language was the common source of Sanskrit, Prakit, Zend, Persian, and Armenian in Asia; and of the Greek, Italic, Celtic, Teutonic, and Slavonic languages in Europe. In like manner their religion gave root to others, which thrived in the fruitful soil of Asia, but have now disappeared in Europe, although traces still remain there in languages, legends, and superstitions.

The Aryans, who entered India, came by way of Persia and, after sojourning on the banks of the Indus, advanced to the east of the Punjab, where they formed a large settlement near the sacred river Sarasvati (Sarusti) in the neighbourhood of Kurukshetra (Thanesar). They afterwards spread into the Gangetic plains and the whole of Central India ; hence the classical name for that portion of India, which lies between the Himalaya and the Vindya mountains, is Arya-Varta, or 'Abode of Aryans.' Another name for India—and that commonly used in Sanskrit literature—is Bharata or Bharata-Varsha, *i.e.*, the 'Country of King Bharata,' a monarch who probably reigned over extensive territories in ancient times.

The Indo-Aryans finally forced their way south of the Vindya mountains and, forming fresh colonies, introduced their customs into all parts of India ; at the same time adopting some of the practices of the earlier races with whom they came into contact.

The aboriginal, or non-Aryan, tribes were looked down upon as savages by the Aryan invaders, and those who did not retreat before them into the forests and mountains were treated as inferior beings and became serfs.

There is reason to believe that the region of the River Sarasvati is the birth-place of Brahmanism or the Hindu religion, but its principal development took place at Benares on the Ganges.

It was in the neighbourhood of Benares that Gautama Buddha commenced his public teaching about 500 B. C. and, for more than a thousand years, the religion, started by him, continued to be a menace to Brahmanism. The great ruler Asoka gave an enormous impetus to Buddhism by appointing it as a State religion and by taking infinite pains to purify its doctrines and spread them abroad. Although many of its principles are still apparent in Hinduism and a sect of Hindus, termed Jains, remain influenced by it, yet Buddhism was not destined to stay in India; between 700 and 900 A.D. it lost ground in the country as a popular faith and finally succumbed to Brahmanism; but it found a permanent footing in Ceylon, Tibet, Nepal, Burma, China, and Japan and is now followed in these countries by millions of people. In a somewhat similar manner the Christian religion, which arose in Palestine, left its birth-place to spread over Europe.

In 337 B.C. an invasion of India by the Greeks, under Alexander the Great, took place from the north-west; it failed, however, to proceed beyond the limits of the Punjab and the Greeks did not remain there long enough to influence the religions of the country; even their successors, the Græco-Bactrians, who occupied the Western Punjab for a considerable period, left little more than their coins to tell the tale.

From about 100 B.C. to 500 A.D. further incursions of tribes, known as Scythians, from Central Asia occurred; these people ousted the Græco-Bactrians and took possession of a tract, which extended from Agra and Sindh in the south to Merve and Yarkand beyond the Himalayas in the north. They adopted the Buddhist faith and their great king, Kanishka, in 40 A.D. established it, with some alteration, as the State religion for the north, just as Asoka had done previously for the south. These invaders were finally subdued by the Indian monarchies of Central India, but many of their descendants exist in the north-west of India and they now profess either the Hindu or the Muslim religion.

About 717 A.D. the Parsees, a small tribe of Persians, were expelled from their native land by followers of the Muslim Khalif Omar and settled in India near Surat, where they became great merchants and men of business. They brought with them the records of their faith—the Zend-Avesta of their prophet Zoroaster—and to this day have adhered to many practices of the ancient religion of Persia, retaining fire as the symbol of the Supreme Being.

Thereafter, at different periods, came conquering hordes of Arabs, Turks, Afghans, Moguls, and Persians from the north-west ; they introduced Islam into the northern regions of India, from Peshawar to Delhi and thence into Bengal. The Muslims frequently became supreme politically, but were never able to convert more than a small proportion of the Hindus and, indeed, they took from them, in language, habits, and character, more perhaps than they imparted.

In the fifteenth century a Hindu reformer named Nanak preached new doctrines in the Punjab and started the religious sect since known as "Sikhs."

The Dutch, Portuguese, and French have all, at one time or another, obtained some territory in India and signs of their influence may still be found at isolated points.

Finally the British gained supremacy throughout the whole of India, including Burma, and the political sway of the British Government is greater than that ever wielded by any former power which has ruled in India.

Notwithstanding the changes throughout all these ages, the greater portion of the population has remained Hindu and the moral influence of Indo-Aryan civilization is still paramount among the masses of India.

In the descriptions which follow, therefore, more space will be allotted to the Hindu religion than to any other.

CHAPTER II.

BELIEFS OF THE ABORIGINALS AND OF THE ARYANS.

Aboriginal Beliefs.

VERY little has been ascertained concerning the manners and customs of the pre-Aryan tribes. Being illiterate, they left no records of any description; indeed, the only sources of information regarding their religion are the Vedic poems (wherein, however, they are described as inferiors, evil livers, and demons), the remains found in tombs, and, finally, deductions from the customs and languages of the existing tribes descended from them.

Throughout the ages there has been considerable amalgamation of the Aryan and the aboriginal elements in blood, language, and religion; but it is possible for one well versed in the Hindu scriptures to distinguish between the early beliefs and those of purely Aryan origin, or introduced by Brahmans. Naturally much information can be obtained in the wilder regions where the ancient tribes are found in something approaching their primitive purity.

The evidence, obtained in this manner, tends to show that the pre-Aryans believed in a vague pantheism, in which all nature was regarded as pervaded by evil spirits, to be appeased by offerings. To these influences were attributed disease and sickness among man and beast; blights and pests among crops; storms and floods; accidents and ill-luck of every description.

Residents in the mountains were under the impression that in each peak dwelt a spirit which must be propitiated by gifts before they commenced cultivation on the hill slopes. The principal crops had special gods, who required satisfaction before sowing or reaping began. There were demons of the forests and those of the streams, all of whom were respected, or rather feared; woe to him who made a clearance in the former and did not leave a clump of trees as a refuge for the mystery god, or who diverted the whole of a rivulet for the irrigation of his land and made no allowance for the thirsty water-nymph.

Then there were the disagreeable and spiteful ghosts of departed ancestors, for the laying of which various ceremonies had to be performed; such as enticing them into the bodies of animals which, after being protected for some time, were finally buried.

It does not appear that any of these malignant powers were represented by images; idolatry seems to have been a production of Hinduism and the aboriginals were probably only too glad to keep their gods at a distance. The nearest approach to idol worship was the marking of certain spots with bright pigment, or the piling of stones round the foot of a tree, to localise the gods, as it were, by symbols.

Witchcraft was evidently practised for the purpose of exercising evil spirits, or for interpreting signs and omens ; we can well believe that something of the kind must have been necessary to relieve the feelings of those unfortunate people.

The religion of the primitive tribes was, in effect, a most uncomfortable one, impregnated with the fear of innumerable evil spirits. It is a fact that many of their descendants of the present day have no knowledge of any omnipotent and beneficent deity, nor do they believe in friendly and cheerful gods, but devote their energies to appease hosts of demons by means of offerings and sacrifices. It is also remarkable that nearly all of their beliefs are still to be found, in one shape or another, among the lower class Hindus or Sudras, and a great many among the rustic population.

Aryan Beliefs.

It is pleasing to turn from these primitive peoples to the almost civilized Aryans, of whose religion we gain such an extensive knowledge from the ancient collection of hymns known as the Rig Veda. This valuable memorial shows them in their early settlements on the banks of the Indus and Sarasvati ; they were happy in possessing bright and lively gods, with none of the malignant fiends which worried the wild tribes whom they found in India.

Our Aryan forefathers in their Asiatic homes appear to have believed originally in an all-pervading spirit, who controlled the universe and regulated the action of the heavenly bodies, but they came to regard each of the principal forces of nature as a separate deity to be invoked as occasion arose. Their houses, lands, and herds were frequently at the mercy of wind, fire, and water; so the forces of the sky and air provided most of their mythology.

Several of the gods of the Indo-Aryans were likewise the gods of the Greeks and Romans and of the ancient Persians; thus Dyaus, the 'sky' or 'heavenly father,' was the Zeus of Greece, the Jupiter (Dyaus-Pitar) of Rome and the old god Tiu of our Tuesday. Aditi was a goddess closely connected with Dyaus, she being the 'boundless expanse' and 'mother of all gods'; while a development of the same called Varuna, the 'encompassing sky,' corresponded with the Roman Uranus and the Ahura Mazda, or Ormazd, of the Zoroastrian mythology.

Varuna was perhaps the greatest of their gods in Central Asia; he was supposed to rule the universe and guide all the forces of nature; he was "all-knowing" and "all-powerful," and a god who would reward the good and punish the evil-doers.

Indra, the god of rain, was more appreciated by the Indo-Aryans, for in Northern India the rainy season has always been looked forward to by agriculturists and its approach hailed by them with delight. This god corresponds with the Jupiter Pluvius of the Romans and for some time took precedence of most others in India, being described as a "mighty warrior, whose arrows of lightning and thunderous roars drove all enemies before him"; he delighted in offerings of strong liquor and was more of a companion than Varuna, the good and just, who somewhat overawed the people.

Agni (Ignis), the god of fire, was a homely deity, who provided warmth in the cold season, repelled darkness and enemies in the shape of wild beasts, and carried the offerings of *ghee* (clarified butter) in flames towards the heavens.

Surya, the sun, gave light and warmth during the day and ripened the crops. Ushas, the dawn, always fresh, fair, and young, provided food for the poet's sweetest songs; while the two Asvinas, or early morning streaks of light, were praised as heralds of the dawn.

One of the most remarkable things to be deified was *Soma,* an intoxicating drink made from the fermented juice of a milky weed (sarcostemma viminale), which grows in the hills. After its discovery it was at first used on occasions of religious ceremonies, but it was lauded and praised to such an extent that finally it attained the position of a god. It was the *Homa* of the Iranians.

Vayu, the wind, and Maruts, the storm gods, complete the list of the principal deities of the Aryans. Curiously enough, the moon and stars received little attention from them and even the goddess Prithvi, the earth, was not given a prominent place; perhaps she was too solid and placid a body to interest these enterprising people.

Before the Aryans entered India they did not apparently make use of idols in their religious ceremonies, nor did they indulge in hero worship. They believed that Yama was the first man and an offspring of the sun, also that on his death he resided in the heavens, where he received and watched over the departed ones. Prayers were said to the spirits of the *pitris* (deceased ancestors), which did not, however, take the spiteful form assigned to them by the primitive Indians.

There were no temples or buildings for public worship in those times, nor did regular priests officiate at the religious ceremonies ; the head of each household performed these duties, which consisted of offering gifts to the gods, praying, and repeating hymns of praise.

Animals, such as goats, sheep, cows and bulls, and even horses, were sacrificed and these, with the *soma,* were considered to augment the strength and activity of the gods.

It is said that the sacrifice of human beings occasionally occurred, but, if so, the practice was uncommon and looked upon with disdain as being a custom of the savages.

It seems that, when they had been settled for some time in the north-west of India, many of the Aryans found time for the study of religious and philosophical matters. They indulged in romance regarding the performances of their ancestors and found food for reflection in the superstitions and fears of the Sudras ; forms of ritual and new gods were created ; not only were the main forces of nature worshipped, but gradually all the feelings, passions, and faculties of the mind became personified and deified ; remarkable objects became regarded as manifestations of the gods ; departed heroes devolved into incarnations of the Almighty. The most extraordinary fables and legends, founded perhaps on outlines of fact, were related regarding the deified personages.

This was the state of affairs which existed when the Indo-Aryans had been settled for several centuries on the banks of the Sarasvati. It was there that the Rig Veda was composed ; there the system of Brahmanism arose ; and there the complicated religion of Hinduism originated.

CHAPTER III.

THE SACRED BOOKS OF THE HINDUS.

THE Hindu scriptures may be divided into two main portions, namely, the 'Inspired,' or *Sruti* (that which has been heard), and the 'Un-inspired,' or *Smriti* (that which has been remembered).

The *Sruti* is supposed to have been divinely uttered and is therefore authoritative; its various parts were handed down by repetition and finally committed to writing by the priests or Brahmans.

The *Smriti* does not rank as direct revelation from the gods, but is classed as sacred tradition.

Some of the ancient literature, however, occupies a middle position and is considered to have been partly inspired; to this category belong the two epic poems, the *Mahabharata* and *Ramayana*; the Hindus also regard their ancient codes of law, or *Dharm Shastras*, as almost divine productions.

The main idea which permeates their scriptures is that there is one pervading Divine Spirit, who manifests himself in miscellaneous ways; there is no hell, such as that mentioned in the Christian scriptures, but the soul passes from one body to another—even into those of animals—receiving reward or punishment in this world, until it finally merges in the Divine Spirit and reaches *Nirvana* or the 'highest heaven.'

Sruti.

The inspired literature consists of the four Vedas and their appendices the Brahmanas.

The word *Veda* means 'knowledge,' and is derived from the root *vid;* it corresponds with the Latin *videre,* 'to see': the English 'to wit': and the Scandinavian *vedan.*

The four Vedas, comprising what is generally termed the "Veda," are called respectively :—The *Rich,* or *Rig Veda;* the *Saman,* or *Sama Veda;* the *Yajush,* or *Yujar Veda;* and the *Atharvana* or *Atharva Veda.* Each of these is now composed of three parts: the *Mantras,* which are hymns of praise in verse; the *Brahmanas,* ritualistic precepts in prose; and the *Upanishads,* commentaries partly in prose and partly in verse, including the *Aranyakas.*

The *Rig Veda* was probably composed about 1500 B.C. and thereafter recited orally until it was reduced to writing; it contains 1,017 poems or hymns of praise, which give a vivid picture of the religion, customs, and manners of the Aryans in their first settlement in the north-west of India and glimpses of their earlier beliefs in Central Asia. Its principal gods have already been mentioned. We can perceive in it signs of a religion which perhaps commenced with monotheism—touched with a dash of pantheism—and gradually relapsed into polytheism, but there is nothing to show that images were worshipped, nor is any mention made of transmigration of souls, or of caste in its Brahmanized form.

The *Sama Veda* and *Yujar Veda* are not of the same importance ; they both contain much of the Rig Veda, arranged for the purposes of ritual, and correspond with the Christian prayer-book.

The *Atharva Veda* is a collection of hymns and was partly compiled from the later portion of the Rig Veda ; it, however, introduces evil divinities, mysteries, spells for dealing with demons, and other practices of a like nature. This work was evidently composed after the Aryans had come into contact with the previous occupants of the country.

To each of the Vedas was attached a commentary called *Brahmana*. It is clear that the priestly class had been formed and had assumed considerable power over the minds of the people, when these were compiled about 600 B.C., for, besides explaining the duties of the priests and the manners in which they are to make sacrifices and perform other rites, they extol their position.

In the divinely inspired portion of the Hindu scriptures, therefore, the *Vedas* supply the hymns of praise or psalms and the *Brahmanas* provide the ritual.

Smriti.

To the inspired Vedas and Brahmanas were afterwards added further sacred works, which are treated as *Smriti*, the 'things remembered.'

We may first mention the *Upanishads* or 'dissolution of ignorance,' which are to be found with various parts of the scriptures, some among the Vedas, many with the Brahmanas and Aranyakas, others standing alone. Only a few were composed in Vedic days and many are of comparatively recent date. There are about 240 of them and they consist of speculative notes regarding God, the soul, and existence. They form the root, as it were, of Hindu philosophy, and practically constitute the only Veda for all thoughtful Hindus of the present time.

There are two ideas of sacred knowledge in the Upanishads. In *Karma Kanda*, the one God, although really without shape, assumes various forms in order to bring himself to the level of human understanding (like the Son of Man). In the other, called *Jnana Kanda*, if true knowledge is to be obtained, one must believe in one great Spirit, who pervades and constitutes the universe, and into whom the souls of men finally merge.

In order to show how union with the Divine Spirit may be obtained, the Upanishads teach *moksha*, or the forgetting of self and surroundings; some seek to achieve this by *Yoga*, which consists of certain physical and mental processes.

The intense religious thinking which had been going on in those early days led persons to become ascetics, who retired to solitary places for meditation and the performance of austerities; for them special appendices of the Vedas, called *Aranyakas*, or 'treatises for the forest recluse,' were compiled.

As time progressed it was considered expedient to classify the former sacred works and commentaries, and to expound philosophical ideas and religious doctrines; thus a series of six treatises, called *Darsanas*, or 'reflections of wisdom,' came to be indited. They were written in *sutras* or *shastras* (strings of aphorisms), based chiefly on the Upanishads, and are as follows:—

1. The Nyaya, founded by Gautama or Akshapada.
2. The Vaiseshika, by Kanada or Kanabhaksha.
3. The Sankhya, by Kapila.
4. The Yoga, by Patanjali.
5. The Mimansa, by Jaimini.
6. The Vedanta, by Badarayana or Vyasa.

The *Nyaya* is an analysis which teaches the method of eliciting true knowledge and of attaining complete happiness. It holds that the world is made up of eternal atoms; that the soul and mind are separate. Although admitting that God has strength, will, and knowledge, yet it does not acknowledge him as all-powerful or as the Creator. Notwithstanding all this the Nyaya supports the truth of the Veda.

The *Vaiseshika* generally follows the Nyaya in its doctrines, but it makes no mention of God.

The *Sankhya* is a system with somewhat agnostic tendency, for it holds that the existence of God is not proved; it declares that there are two eternal agencies—Nature and Souls; three principles—Truth, Passion, and Darkness; it also mentions that "out of nothing can nothing come."

None of the above three systems contemplate prayer or worship as necessary.

The *Yoga* agrees with the Sankhya in almost every particular, but curiously differs in acknowledging the existence of a Supreme Being; it propounds the extraordinary doctrine that, in order to effect union with God, it is necessary to concentrate the mind on one special matter or object. Followers of this system are called Yogis and may be seen assuming curious postures and performing awful austerities.

The *Mimansa* is a kind of scientific disquisition on the Veda, which is pronounced to be the only truth.

The *Vedanta* means the 'end of the Veda' and therefore should be an analysis, but actually it is a philosophical discussion founded on supplementary works like the Upanishads. In the Vedanta system God, who is one with the soul, pervades the universe. Meditation is considered to be the great requisite, for thereby true knowledge is acquired and it is declared that "he who knows God becomes God"; when this is stated, it is difficult to follow the conclusions regarding transmigration.

Sankara Acharya, a disciple of Kumarila and native of Malabar, during extensive wanderings, preached regarding the Vedanta system with so much success that he popularized it among those of both high and low caste, leaving on his death a compact sect among the Brahmans and a popular religion; for Siva, in his capacity as destroyer and creator, appealed to the priestly class and, in his terrible shapes, was a suitable deity to attract the Sudras and non-Aryan races with their religion of fear.

Another philosophical compilation of some importance, which may be noted here, is the *Bhagavat Gita*, which is inserted in the middle of the Mahabharata. It deals, to a large extent, with the views expressed in the Yoga, Sankhya, and Vedanta systems and attempts to bring them into harmony. Much of this work is taken up with a dialogue between Krishna and Arjuna, one of the great leaders mentioned in the Mahabharata. Considerable respect is shown for the words uttered by Krishna, for he is supposed to have been a manifestation of the great god Vishnu. The existence of an external world is admitted and the book teaches the advantages of concentrating the mind. It avoids magic and asceticism, and is principally concerned in the laudation of Krishna, who is regarded as the Supreme Being and is described as finally revealing himself to Arjuna in this capacity—possessed of myriads of faces with features shining like the sun. A noticeable feature of the work is the similarity, in certain respects, of the story of Krishna to that of Christ in the New Testament.

The Puranas.

The name *Purana* means 'old tradition.' Most of the Puranas, generally believed to be eighteen in number, were compiled probably about 1000 and 1100 A. D. Their names are :—(1) Brahma; (2) Padma; (3) Vishnu; (4) Siva; (5) Bhagavata; (6) Narada; (7) Markandeya; (8) Agni; (9) Bhavishya; (10) Brahma Vaivarta; (11) Linga; (12) Varaha; (13) Skanda; (14) Vamana; (15) Kurma; (16) Matsya; (17) Garuda; (18) Brahmanda.

Numbers 2, 3, 5, 6, 10, 12, and 17 are in favour of Vishnu; numbers 4, 8, 11, 13, 15, and 16 praise Siva; number 14 extols both Vishnu and Siva; while number 9 respects the triad, Brahma, Vishnu, and Siva.

Each Purana is supposed to treat of the following five subjects :—

1. The original creation.
2. The destruction and re-creation of the universe.
3. The genealogy of gods and patriarchs.
4. The reigns and periods of the Manus.
5. The history of the solar and lunar races of kings.

They actually seem to be a religious encyclopædia, in which the various doctrines and legends relating to Brahma, but more especially to Vishnu and Siva, were brought together.

The Bhagavata is one of the most popular of the Puranas; it exalts the favourite god Vishnu in the form of Krishna, who is also called 'Bhagavat,' and there is an account of his life in the tenth book, a version of which, in Hindi, is the well-known *Prem-Sagar* or 'Ocean of Love.'

There are also eighteen *Upa-Puranas*, which deal with the same matters as the Puranas and were written later as their appendices.

The Hindu Trinity.

In the Veda mention is occasionally made of the triple form of fire and of the three gods Agni, Surya, and Indra as a kind of joint manifestation; later the doctrine of a trinity, or rather triple manifestation, developed. Brahmă, the universal and Supreme Being, assumed the form of "activity" as Brahmā the Creator, of "goodness" as Vishnu the Preserver, and of "darkness" as Siva the Destroyer. This formation first appears in the Brahmanized version of the Indian epics. The Vedic Vishnu, connected with Surya, the sun, became Vishnu the preserver; Rudra, connected with Indra and the Maruts, became the destroyer Siva.

According to Hindu belief all death leads to new life, all destruction to reproduction; hence Siva finally becomes the creator and he is more often symbolized by *Linga*, the male organ of generation and emblem of reproduction, than by any representation of destruction. Sometimes the *linga* is surrounded by the female symbol *Yoni*.

Vishnu and Siva, in their various male and female shapes, have continued to be the favourite gods of the Hindu.

Lakhshmi, or Sri, the goddess of wealth, is Vishnu's wife or counterpart and, as such, brings out all his kindly qualities ; Kali, the wife of Siva, on the other hand, is a terrible goddess, who exercises all his destructive power and requires a vast amount of propitiation.

Vishnu is said to have ten *ăvătars*, or descents, as follows :—

1. *Matsya*, Fish.
2. *Kurma*, Tortoise.
3. *Varaha*, Boar.
4. *Nara Sinha*, Man-lion.
5. *Vamana*, Dwarf.
6. *Parasu Rama.*
7. *Rama*, of the Ramayana.
8. *Krishna.*
9. *Gautama Buddha.*
10. *Kalki*—yet to appear.

The first three have reference to a great deluge, such as is referred to in the scriptures of most religions. The Hindu account of this flood is that Manu, the second ancestor of mankind, received orders from the Almighty to construct a ship and take with him therein seven holy men and seeds of all living beings. When the waters rose, Vishnu in the shape of Matsya, an enormous fish, appeared and towed it to a high peak where it rested until the flood subsided. In the form of Kurma, a tortoise, he recovered during the deluge many valuable articles from the bottom of the sea, including the beautiful goddess Lakhshmi, the wife of Vishnu.

In his third appearance as Varaha, a boar, Vishnu fought with a terrible demon named Hiranyaksha and raised the earth, which had been thrown into a gulf by his opponent.

In the fourth descent a demon king, Hiranya Kashyapu, had obtained a promise from Brahmā that no god, man, nor animal should have power to slay him, but when he attempted to destroy his own son Prahlad, who displeased him by respecting Vishnu, the latter suddenly appeared in the shape, not of god, man, or beast, but of Nara-Sinha, a man-lion, and tore him to pieces.

As Vamana, a dwarf, in his fifth descent Vishnu requested a king named Bali, who was scheming to displace Indra from his dominion, to give him as much of his territory as he could stride over in three paces; on the gift being granted, he suddenly assumed enormous proportions and, taking heaven and earth with his first two steps, placed his foot on Bali and crushed him into the nether regions with the third.

The sixth descent was as Parasu Rama, who proceeded throughout the earth slaying Kshatriyas with an axe, because they had been ill-treating Brahmans. Parasu Rama dwelt near Goa, but shame of his mother's misdeeds made him leave that place and it is said that, in his anger, he seized a battle-axe and hurled it from the mountains southwards across the sea as far as Cape Comorin. The consequence was that the ocean there dried up and became the long flat tract of country now called Malabar. The battle-axe used to figure on the ancient coinage of the West Coast of India.

The seventh was one of Vishnu's most celebrated incarnations; he then appeared in the form of

Rama, or Ram Chandra, the romantic story of whom is related separately.

When Vishnu descended for the eighth time, it was to appear in the shape of the popular Krishna. The legend runs that Kansa, once king of Mathura (Muttra), imprisoned a person named Vasudeva and his wife Devati, because of a prophecy that one of their sons would slay him ; he killed off six of the sons in succession as they were born, but the seventh escaped by a miracle. Vasudeva contrived also to get away with his eighth son, the wondrous Krishna, the 'dark one.' The infant, who was placed in charge of a herdsman called Nanda, soon began to distinguish himself by his miraculous powers and by his capacity for joking and amusement. Many are the tales of his sports with the *Gopis*, or milkmaids, on the banks of the Jumna ; he hid their garments while they bathed, purloined their milk and butter, and indeed played all kinds of pranks with the women-folk. He was also not satisfied with a thousand wives but indulged in six times that number.

Krishna is frequently represented as a young man with a black face, standing on one foot with the other crossed and only the points of the toes touching the ground ; in this position he plays a flute.

Krishna appears in the Mahabharata as a distinguished prince and, after going through the great war between the Pandavas and Kauravas, finally falls a victim to the flight of an arrow shot by an archer who mistakes him for a deer.

Buddha is regarded as the ninth incarnation and it is related that Vishnu assumed this shape to deceive low-caste people, or demons, into neglecting the worship of the gods.

In the tenth *ăvătar*, which is yet to come at the end of the present or *Kali* age, Vishnu is expected to appear as Kalki, for the purpose of punishing the wicked, destroying the enemies of Brahmans, and re-establishing righteousness upon earth. It is said that he will be revealed in the sky, mounted on a white steed, with a flaming sword in his hand.

The Tantras.

The Tantras contain doctrines which form the creed of a comparatively small class called *Tantrikăs*. Many of the principles, when acted upon, are especially liable to develop impurity and licentiousness.

A Tantra is supposed to treat of five subjects :—

1. Creation.
2. Destruction.
3. Worship of gods.
4. Attainment of the final object.
5. Four modes of union with the Supreme Spirit.

They are not, however, confined to these points, but include evil spells, magic, witchcraft, with many other matters of mystery. Altogether they form a very low class of literature.

A large number of Tantras have been written and they take the place of the Puranas for a class known as *Saktas*, or worshippers of the *Sakti*. The meaning of this word is the energy-giving will, or power, of the three gods Brahmā, Vishnu, and Siva, as manifested in their wives. Sarasvati is the wife of Brahmā, and Lakhshmi, or Sri, that of Vishnu; but it is Kali, the female counterpart of Siva, who is especially responsible for the more horrible and repulsive practices. Kali is also known as Durga, Parvati, Devi, Bhairavi, Uma, and by other names.

The Tantras urge secrecy upon those who practise Sakti rites.

The Saktas, of whom further mention is made in Chapter XI, are mostly left-hand worshippers, that is, they select the goddesses— whose images are always placed on the left of the gods—for special attention.

CHAPTER IV.

BRAHMANS, CASTE, AND THE DHARM SHASTRAS.

THE Aryans probably had no systematic arrangement of classes before they arrived in India. It would appear that they were divided into tribes, each of which had its selected chieftain who controlled the tribal affairs of all kinds, while the head of each family group acted as captain and priest within the tribe.

When they abandoned their nomadic life and settled in the Punjab many took to agriculture; some engaged in trade and handicrafts; others practised military exercises and acted as warriors for the protection of the settlements against assault, or for waging war to acquire fresh territory. To supply the want of menials they made slaves of the prisoners whom they took from among the aboriginals.

After a time, the more intellectual Aryans began to constitute themselves the religious teachers and political guides of the people, becoming known as *Brahmans* or 'divine ones.' They framed stringent rules to ensure their position and before long, owing to their superior knowledge and intelligence, gained enormous influence over all others and monopolized the spiritual authority.

The Brahmans taught that the deity regards human beings as unequal; that different kinds of men are created, just as there are various species of animals. Members of the superior classes however, by means of transmigration of souls, are to be born again in a higher or lower status, according to their good or bad actions during life, and this occurrence will be continually repeated until at length each soul becomes united with Brahmă.

It was in this manner that the present vast and intricate system of caste came into existence. The English word "caste" is believed to have been derived from the Portuguese *casta*, meaning breed or strain, and caste is now hereditary.

The four main castes, as announced by the Brahmans in the ancient law books of the Hindus, were :—

1. The *Brahmans*, or priestly class.
2. The *Kshatriya*, or military class.
3. The *Vaisya*, or agricultural and later the trading class.
4. The *Sudra*, or servile class.

The first three constituted the twice-born and obtained a second spiritual birth (like baptism) by investiture with a sacred thread, whilst the Sudras were only once-born outsiders and inferior creatures.

The Brahman was the lord of all, for he proceeded from the mouth of the Creator and possessed the right to study, teach, and expound the holy Veda; it was through him alone that the wishes and commands of the gods were revealed and he constituted, as it were, the divine agent upon earth.

The fighting Kshatriya appropriately issued from Brahmā's mighty arm; the food-providing Vaisya from his sinewy thigh; and the down-trodden Sudra from his foot.

The four original classes gradually became sub-divided to suit social, geographical, and religious conditions and at the present time castes may be counted in thousands; the second and third classes have lost their original significance, but the Brahman reigns supreme and the mainstay of Brahmanism is caste. Every good Hindu looks forward to attain a higher position in his next life, until finally his soul, thoroughly purified, enters the great Brahmă, the divine essence which pervades the whole universe.

In the south of India some of the Sudra, or aboriginal, castes have succeeded in obtaining recognition as Brahmans; they wear the sacred thread and refuse precedence to the admitted Brahmans.

The late Sir Denzil Ibbetson in summarizing his learned disquisition on caste in the "Report on the Census of the Punjab, 1881," remarks:—

"Thus if the theory be correct, we have the following steps in the process by which caste has been evolved in the Punjab:—

(1) The tribal divisions common to all primitive societies;

(2) the guilds based upon hereditary occupation common to the middle life of all communities;

(3) the exaltation of the priestly office to a degree unexampled in other countries ;

(4) the exaltation of the Levitical blood by a special insistence upon the necessarily hereditary nature of occupation ;

(5) the preservation and support of this principle by the elaboration from the theories of the Hindu creed or cosmogony of a purely artificial set of rules, regulating marriage and inter-marriage, declaring certain occupations and foods to be impure and polluting, and prescribing the conditions and degree of social intercourse permitted between the several castes. Add to these the pride of social rank and the pride of blood which are natural to man, and which alone could reconcile a nation to restrictions at once irksome from a domestic and burdensome from a material point of view ; and it is hardly to be wondered at that caste should have assumed the rigidity which distinguishes it in India."

Mention has been made of the strict rules which were framed by the Brahmans ; these were not only for the regulation of religious rites and practices, but also for the administration of justice and the control of domestic affairs. They favoured the Brahman throughout and kept the castes apart by prohibiting members of one eating and drinking with, or marrying, those of another ; they dealt minutely with the duties to be performed by each class in their daily life and especially laid down those for the Brahmans through each stage of their existence.

The rules were recorded in more than fifty codes of law, called *Dharm Shastras*, or *Sutras*. About twenty are still extant and, of these, the *Code of Manu*, compiled, or at any rate commenced, before the Christian era, is by far the most important ; the *Yajṇavalkya Code* takes the second place and follows the main principles of its predecessor.

The Code of Manu contains twelve books and their subjects are conveniently classified under six heads :—

1. *Veda*—true knowledge and religion.
2. *Vedanta* or *Atmavidya*—general philosophy.
3. *Acara*—established custom, including caste observances, the divisions of a Brahman's life and domestic ceremonies.
4. *Vyavahara*—monarchical government, civil and criminal law.
5. *Prayas-chit*—rules of penance.
6. *Kărm-phăl*—consequence of acts, transmigration.

On the occasion of every religious and domestic ceremony the Hindu is required by these laws to make an offering to the Brahmans and he is led to believe that his death at an especially holy place, such as Benares, Hardwar, or Kurukshetra, will result in his immediate elevation to a higher caste, or even in his absorption at once into the Great Essence. It is the duty of Hindus to contribute towards the cost of construction or upkeep of holy edifices, bathing-ghats, and the like. By these means sacred places are maintained, and the priestly class receive their sustenance.

The following twelve *Sănskārās*, or purificatory rites, are prescribed in Manu for cleansing a person from hereditary sin :—

1. *Garbhadhana*, the ceremony on conception.
2. *Punsavana*, on first indication of pregnancy.
3. *Simantomayana*, arranging the mother's hair.
4. *Jata-karman*, feeding an infant with honey and *ghee* at birth.
5. *Nama-karana*, naming on the tenth or twelfth day after birth.
6. *Nish-kramana*, taking the child out to see the sun and moon in the 4th month.
7. *Anna-prasana*, feeding the infant with rice between the 5th and 8th month.
8. *Cuda-karman*, or *Caula*, tonsure, except one lock on the crown, in the 2nd or 3rd year.
9. *Upanayana*, investiture with the sacred thread.
10. *Kesanta*, cutting off the hair, of a Brahman at 16, of a Kshatriya at 22, and of a Vaisya at 24 years of age.

11. *Samavartana*, when a student returns home after completing his studies under a *guru*.
12. *Vivaha*, marriage.

These are not all fully observed and, while numbers 7 and 12 are the only rites to which Sudras are admitted by the codes, several of the others are practised by them.

The *Cuda-karman* leaves the young child with that remarkable little lock of hair (*sikha* in Sanskrit, *choti* in Hindi, or *kudumi* in Tamil) on the crown of the head, which is the distinguishing feature of most Hindus.

The top of the head is regarded as sacred and as the residence of the deity in the human body and the central point is sometimes known as the "top eye." That spot has also been thought to be the fountain or source of the generating power of man, and the tuft of hair is left so that it may remain covered and safe from defilement. Certain *Sannyasis*, however, keep their heads entirely bald, for they declare that they are in union with God and therefore the spot requires no protection; they also discard the sacred thread for the same reason.

When a Hindu child is born the father will sometimes sprinkle water with his own tuft into the mouth of the infant before looking at or handling it.

The shaving or tonsure of the child's head is an important religious ceremony. An astrologer is consulted to fix an auspicious day. During its performance cocoanuts and bananas are offered to an image of Ganesha (Pillayar), son of Siva (Iswara), and cocoanut juice is sprinkled over the hair, beginning with the central point; the liquid so used being presented as an offering to Parvati, the consort of Siva. The hair shaven off is placed by some in a silver locket which is tied to the child's waist as an amulet against disease; by others it is preserved in an earthenware pot.

If a succession of children die, the next one will have his tuft kept at the back of the head and finally, if he survives, it will be removed and another allowed to grow in the usual position.

On the occasion of the death of a married man his heir cuts off the top-knot, in order to uncover the sacred spot, and places a pot of water upon it to preserve the soul of the departed.

The top of the head and the hair have been regarded as sacred from very ancient times, and rites in connection therewith are mentioned in the scriptures of most religions.

In former days chiefs suspended scalps, to which the *sikha* was attached, to their horses' bridles and the Scythians used to carry those of the men they had killed in battle in this manner in order to claim their share of booty. A warrior, with such a decoration on his bridle, was regarded as a hero, and this is probably the origin of the *kuzi*, or ornament consisting of bunches of hair, which, hanging below the bridle, forms part of the accoutrements of an officer's charger in a cavalry regiment even to this day.

The *Upanayana*, or investiture with the sacred thread, is performed on Brahmans in their eighth year and on others at a later age. The sacred cord (*jănnu*) of a Brahman must be of cotton and consist of three threads (*tri-vrit*) twisted to the right ; that of others is made of hemp or wool with the same number of threads. The ceremony for a Brahman is somewhat as follows :—

The boy faces the sun and then walks thrice round the fire ; after this, he is taught by a Brahman to make three suppressions of the breath, to say "*Om*," to repeat the mystical words *Bhur*, *Bhuvar*, and *Suvar* (this world, the middle region, and heaven) and to recite the following prayer—"Let us contemplate the divine splendour of the sun-god, the donor of bliss to all ; that he may give us every kind of happiness in the whole world." The thread is thereupon placed over his head and, being supported by the left shoulder, hangs across the body to the right hip.

The word "Om" is full of mystical significance. Thoughtful Hindus regard it as divine and one to be repeated with holy musing. It is constituted by three impulses of the voice and made up of the sounds A, U (or V), and M. Originally these may have referred to the Vedic deities Agni, Varuna, and Mitra ; to some the letters imply the three principal attributes of the Supreme Being, personified as Brahmā, Vishnu, and Siva ; followers of the Vedanta philosophy consider them to mean Creation, Meditation, and Eternal Happiness.

According to the Shastras a Brahman should pass through four stages, or *asrams*, during his life :—

1. A period of studentship lasting for twelve years, during which he must acquire a knowledge of the Veda.
2. Marriage and household duties.
3. Hermitage in the forest.
4. Asceticism and withdrawal from worldly concerns.

There are five sacred fires described in Manu, namely :—*Dakshina, Garhapatya, Ahavaniya, Sabhya,* and *Asavathya.* A Brahman who keeps all of these burning continually is called an *Agnihotri* and is considered very pious.

Although in the present day thousands of Brahmans and other Hindus may be found, who endeavour to follow the precepts of the Shastras, their customs have altered considerably to suit modern conditions, and much is done nowadays which would have meant loss of caste in former times.

We may divide the priests of the present day into four divisions :—The family pastors ; the priests who officiate at temples ; those in charge of monasteries ; and the *gurus* or teachers.

The pastor performs the ceremonies at births, deaths, and marriages ; he grants horoscopes, fixes auspicious dates for harvest operations and other events ; he conducts in fact all kinds of religious rites for families throughout the year ; for each and all of these services payment in cash or kind is made, a fixed allowance being granted sometimes in addition ; he is called the *Parohit* or *Bhat.*

The priest of the temple takes care of the edifice, its idols and furniture ; he performs ceremonies and conducts services connected with the deity or deities to whom it is dedicated and receives offerings on their behalf ; sometimes a considerable amount of property, in land or houses, is attached to a temple, and the head priest will have a large establishment to assist him. In Bengal, the hereditary priest of a Hindu temple is called *Panda* and under him a *pujari* serves.

The head of a monastery is known as a *Mahant* and his disciples as *chelas.* There is a *langar,* or public kitchen, attached to this institution, where the poor are fed ; also a number of quarters in which disciples of the brotherhood can lodge free of charge during their peregrinations.

The *guru* is perhaps the most respected of all personages and sometimes receives homage amounting to deification ; notwithstanding what is written in the Shastras it is now generally understood that any Hindu may qualify for this position and need not necessarily be a Brahman ; it follows that both the highest and the lowest castes have their *gurus* and, as the qualifications are self-imposed, many of them have no title to act as religious teachers or to command esteem.

Women.—In Vedic days women occupied a position of respect ; many of them were intellectual, and some distinguished themselves by composing poetry which has come down to the present day, but a great change came about with the rise of Brahmanism. They were allotted no place among the "twice-born" and although they have "caste" it is merely for social reasons. This is all the more strange because women have a somewhat prominent position in Hindu mythology. To mention a few instances—there are Sarasvati, Lakshmi, and the terrible Kali, goddesses respectively of speech, wealth, and destruction, and wives of the three great gods of the trinity; also the fair and virtuous Sita, famous for all time as the heroine of the Ramayana. In the Code of Manu the gentle sex is given a most inferior position and treated much as the servile class; it allows a woman no right in property; her duty is to marry and bear progeny; she is the slave of man—first under her father, then her husband, and finally under her sons; early marriage is preached and yet a widow may not re-marry.

The *pardah* system, which was borrowed largely from the Musalmans, has provided an existence for Hindu ladies, which is practically lifelong imprisonment and restrains them from exercising mind and body. There is a certain amount of indulgence on occasions of religious gatherings, but it is really only among the rustic and the lower classes that a Hindu woman has any freedom, and even among them the widow is despised and sometimes ill-treated.

During the latter part of the last century, however, efforts were made by some Hindus to advance the status of their womanhood in India, and it is to be hoped that these tiny springs will develop until the tide of knowledge and freedom flows into the *zenanas* throughout this vast and wonderful country.

CHAPTER V.

THE EPIC POEMS.

ACCORDING to legendary history there were originally two great lines of rulers in Northern India, namely, the *Solar* and *Lunar* dynasties.

The Solar kings had their capital at Ayodhya, in the modern province of Oudh, and are said to have originated from the Sun, if not from the divine Brahmā himself. The Lunar monarchs ruled the country to the north-west in the neighbourhood of the present Delhi, and they were believed to have had their descent from the Moon.

Narratives of these royal races are to be found in two famous Epic Poems. One of these, the *Ramayana*, records the wonderful adventures of certain members of the Solar race and deals with an expedition made by them into Southern India and Ceylon ; it consists of about 48,000 lines divided into seven parts, and is said to have been composed by a poet named Valmiki, who is believed to have resided near the confluence of the Ganges and Jumna. The other is the *Mahabharata*, an enormous collection of legends in verse, composed at various times by a number of authors ; it contains about 220,000 lines in eighteen sections, each of which would fill a huge volume, and it forms a cyclopædia of Hindu mythology and philosophy, besides giving a long description of the struggles for supremacy between two branches of the Lunar dynasty.

The Ramayana.

The story runs that King Dasaratha, reigning at Ayodhya, has two sons, Rama and Lakshmana, by his wife Kausalya, and one, named Bharata, by his other wife Kaikeyi.

While Rama is still a youth he enters into a competition to bend the miraculous bow of Siva the Destroyer, which is in the possession of Janaka, king of the neighbouring State of Mithela (North Behar and Tirhut); he proves successful and wins Sita, the king's most beautiful daughter, as his bride, for she is the prize.

Now, in an absent moment, Dasaratha has promised to grant Kaikeyi any two boons which she may desire, and the lady, being jealous of the favoured eldest son Rama, bethinks her of demanding his banishment for fourteen years to the forest of Dandaka and the installation of her son Bharata in his stead. Dasaratha has to comply and directs Rama to leave. The young prince accordingly sets out with his loving wife Sita and his brother Lakshmana, who insists on accompanying them.

Some little time afterwards the sorrowing father dies of grief, and Bharata, who declines to succeed to the throne, goes off in search of Rama; he finds him at Citrakuta on the bank of the river Pisuni, and endeavours to persuade him to return to his kingdom, even offering to continue the banishment in his place. Rama, however, remaining firm, refuses to disobey the order of his deceased father, and insists on completing the fourteen years. At length Bharata goes back to Ayodhya and carries on the government in his brother's name, but he never passes an order without first saluting Rama's shoes, which he has taken with him.

After this, Rama, Sita, and Lakshmana wander about for ten years until one day they meet a sage, named Agastya, in the Vindya Mountains and, acting on his advice, take up their residence at a place called Pancavati on the Godaveri. This neighbourhood is infested with demons, and staying with them is the female demon Surpa-naka, sister of Ravana, the terrible many-headed demon king of Ceylon; unfortunately she falls in love with Rama, and is much annoyed because he rejects her advances. Out of spite she makes an attack upon Sita, but is seen by Lakshmana, who promptly cuts off her nose and ears. Smarting with pain and indignation, Surpa-naka rushes off to her brother, inspires him with a passion for Sita, and incites him to carry her off. This is done by means of a magic aerial car, called "Pushpaka," and the assistance of another demon Marica, who, in the shape of a deer, entices Rama and Lakshmana away, while Ravana in their absence abducts the lovely Sita.

He takes her to Ceylon in his car and there, by means of bribes and threats, attempts to induce her to become his queen, but without avail. At length she is handed over to female demons for starvation and torture, but is sustained throughout this ordeal with nourishment sent by the gods.

Meanwhile, Rama and his brother are making great preparations for her rescue. They first fight and defeat a headless demon named Kabandha, and then make an alliance with Sugriva, king of the monkeys, who lends them his forces, under the command of the monkey-general Hanuman, for the attack on Ravana.

The difficulty of crossing over to Ceylon is overcome by the monkeys, who fly through the air and bring rocks from every direction to form a bridge; even portions of the Himalayas are sent down by the gods and a passage is safely effected.

A battle royal now commences in which the gods all assemble to fight against a mighty array of demons. At a certain stage Rama advances in a chariot specially lent him by Indra, and engages in single combat with the powerful Ravana in his magic car; the two armies stay their fight and look on at the duel, which continues for several days. Rama, after cutting off dozens of heads from his opponent, discovers that others promptly grow in their place and that he is invulnerable in that quarter; nothing daunted, he obtains a thunderbolt from Brahmā and discharges this into the body of his enemy, with the result that the terrible demon-monarch succumbs on the spot and victory is his.

The long-suffering Sita is now recovered and brought back in state to her husband's camp, but he refuses to receive her, because she has become contaminated in Ravana's custody. The lady, however, convinces him of her chastity by walking unharmed through fire, and, full of joy, Rama takes her to his heart.

They mount the aerial car, Pushpaka, and proceed to a spot near Prayag, where they remain until the full period of banishment has expired. Finally they proceed towards home, make a triumphant entry into Ayodhya, where, soon afterwards, Rama is crowned with great pomp and glory, and thereafter rules his people with wisdom and justice.

The Mahabharata.

The main subject of this immense poem is the great contest between the *Pandavas* and *Kauravas*, descendants of King Bharata, a Lunar monarch of great fame.

The introduction of the story is contained in *Adi-parvan*, which relates how two princes, Dhritarashtra and Pandu, are brought up by their uncle Bhishma at Hastinapura, the capital of a province north-east of the present city of Delhi. When the time comes for Pandu to succeed to the throne, he is stricken by a curse and compelled to retire to a hermitage in the Himalayas, so his brother Dhritarashtra reigns in his stead.

Now Pandu leaves behind him five sons, called Pandavas after their father, and his brother has a hundred sons, all of bad character, who are termed Kauravas after an ancestor named Kuru. The two sets of brothers live together under the care of Dhrita-rashtra, but the Kauravas become jealous, because Yudhi-shthira, the eldest of the Pandavas, has been proclaimed heir to the throne. At length they manage to persuade their father to expel their five cousins, who, after wandering in the jungles, arrive at the court of Drupada, king of Panchala. This monarch happens to be holding a tournament (*svayamvara*), and, as was not uncommon in those times, the chief prize is the hand of his daughter, a very beautiful maiden named Draupadi. Arjuna, one of the Pandavas, a great warrior and a youth of much force of character, wins the fair lady, and, curious to relate, she becomes the common wife of the five brothers. (It may be noted that the practice of polyandry exists at the present day among certain hill-tribes in India). Shortly after this event, the Pandavas are recalled from exile and the kingdom is divided between them and the Kauravas; the latter retaining certain territory around Hastinapura and their cousins receiving the province of Indra-prastha (ancient Delhi).

The Kauravas, however, do not leave their relatives in peace; they invite the five brothers to a gambling festival at their capital and then conspire to cheat Yudhi-shthira in a game of dice.

He stakes and loses everything, including his kingdom and even the lady Draupadi. The old father of the wicked Kauravas compels them to restore their immoral gains, but, directly afterwards, further gambling is arranged and it ends by the five brothers with their wife being compelled to retire into banishment for twelve years. This portion of the tale appears in the *Sabha-parvan*, and the adventures during banishment are described in the *Vana-parvan* which follows.

The fourth section, or *Virata-parvan*, relates how the Pandavas enter the service of a king named Virata during the year following the period of their exile. After this, we read in the *Udyoga-parvan*, of the vast preparations made for war between the cousins.

The next four parts of the poem are devoted to a description of the frightful battle which rages for many days between the Kauravas and Pandavas on the Kurukshetra plain ; these sections are named after the Kaurava generals Bhishma, Drona, Karna, and Salya, and enter into minute details as to how they respectively met their deaths.

In the middle of the *Bhishma-parvan* is inserted the *Bhagavad Gita*, which gives an account of the appearance of Krishna upon the scene and of his doings during the struggle ; this poem is of much later date than those of the main story and is given in the form of conversation between the gay god and Arjuna, one of the five Pandavas and their greatest leader. In the remaining sections frequent interpolations regarding Krishna have been made.

The *Salya-parvan* contains a description of the concluding operations of the great fight, when only three of the Kaurava brothers remain alive.

Sauptika-parvan, the tenth part, gives details of a night attack made by the Pandavas, which results in the slaughter of the last three Kauravas.

The next section, *Stri-parvan*, is full of the lamentations of the women-folk and the funeral ceremonies of the departed heroes.

The *Santi-parvan* refers to the coronation of Yudhi-shthira at Hastinapura, and enters into a long series of lectures by Bhishma, who has come to life again, as to the best methods of government and many other matters. These instructions are contained in the *Anusasana*, or thirteenth *parvan*, which towards the end announces the death of Bhishma, the sage and warrior.

The remaining five sections relate how the aged Dhrita-rashtra, with his queen Gandhari, and Kunti, mother of the Pandavas, retires to a forest, where they finally immolate themselves by fire in order to secure salvation; how Krishna and his family meet their end; and how the five Pandavas, with their wife Draupadi, after remarkable adventures, finally make a marvellous ascent into the heaven of Indra. There is a scene when king Yudhi-shthira arrives at the heavenly entrance with his favourite dog; Indra naturally refuses to admit the animal, but he consents on satisfactory proof being furnished that it is really an incarnation of Yama, the first mortal, who has taken this form to protect the hero on earth and later to conduct his soul into heaven.

There is probably a substratum of truth in these two Epic Poems. We can imagine that the Aryans, who moved into the Gangetic plains from the neighbourhood of ancient Delhi and were there ruled by members of the "Solar" dynasty, undertook an expedition against the aboriginals (demons) of Southern India and thence against a savage monarch in Ceylon; also that they vanquished the enemy with the assistance of other primitive tribes (or monkeys), who enabled the invaders by some means or other to cross by way of Adam's Bridge.

It is also likely that two branches of the so-called Lunar dynasty quarrelled over territory and indulged in a bloody conflict in the vicinity of Kurukshetra, where, throughout the history of India, so many decisive battles have been fought.

The exploits of the heroes of these campaigns would naturally have formed the theme for laudatory poems, in which deeds and adventures, already enlarged upon by the returned warriors, were exaggerated with poetical license. These compositions must have received further embellishment as they were recited through centuries, until at length they were recorded by the Brahmans, who gave them additional gloss and, what is more, provided them with religious shape.

CHAPTER VI.

Hindu Domestic Ceremonies.

There are a great many semi-religious ceremonies which have to be performed by Hindus on the birth of children, during childhood, on investiture with the sacred thread, on the occasion of marriage or death, and after the death of near relations.

The purificatory rites required for a Brahman have already been mentioned in Chapter IV, and many of these are now imitated by other castes and classes, while new ceremonies have been introduced from time to time.

Childhood.—On the birth of a child the father holds a reception and presents sugar and sugar-candy to relatives and friends. On the 10th or 12th day the mother is anointed with sesamum oil, after the manner of the Old Testament, and on the same day the child receives its name—perhaps that of one of its ancestors, or one selected to ward off small-pox, or to please one of the gods—it being written by the father three times with a golden ring in unhusked rice spread on a plate. Thereafter money is distributed to the poor, while friends and relatives are entertained. The child is put into a cradle for the first time on the evening of this day, and the guests depart after having blessed the infant and after receiving betel-nut and bananas or other refreshment.

On the birth of a girl there is very little rejoicing, for daughters cannot carry on the ceremonies necessary for their ancestors' souls and they are regarded as expensive luxuries.

At five months of age the ceremony of *choulam* occurs, and the lobes of the ears are pierced with a thin gold ring.

Anna-prasana, or giving rice for the first time, occurs between the fifth and eighth month, and, both then and on the occasion of *choulam*, guests are entertained.

The first birthday is an occasion of festivity; the child is then anointed, decorated with ornaments, and, in the evening, presented to a deity at the local temple.

The shaving of the head, or tonsure, is performed during the second or third year on a propitious day selected by a Brahman after consulting the stars (see Chapter IV).

When a boy is five years old his father fixes a lucky day for the commencement of his teaching and a private instructor is chosen, or he is sent to the local infants' school.

In the seventh or ninth year the youth is invested with the sacred thread, as already described.

These are the principal ceremonies of childhood, but there are many others and, at one and all, Brahmans have to be fed, while it is customary also to entertain friends and relations.

Marriage.—Marriage is a sacred duty for the Hindus, except, of course, for men of those religious sects the rules of which require celibacy ; no ordinary man is considered respectable until he is married, and parents incur the antipathy of the gods and opprobrium in the eyes of their neighbours if they fail to marry off their daughters.

As there are generally more women than men, it is sometimes difficult to secure a suitable husband for a girl ; in fact large sums often have to be paid to do so. What with this and the cost of entertaining friends, relations, and Brahmans, the expenditure more often than not is out of all proportion to the status of the father ; indeed it is quite common for a man to borrow to the full extent of his credit and to mortgage, or even sell, all his property in order to raise a sum, equivalent to several years' income, to squander on the wedding of one of his daughters.

This insane custom has led not only to polygamy, but also to female infanticide, child marriage, and the prohibition of widow re-marriage, while the abhorrent practice of *suttee* (immolation of widows with their deceased husbands) existed until it was prohibited by the British Government.

It has also resulted in an inordinate desire for boys to be born instead of girls, and to every attention being paid to the former while the latter are neglected.

The match-maker for most castes is the family barber, but sometimes a Brahman is employed ;

his duty is to search from house to house for a suitable bride, to carry out preliminary negotiations and to assist at the festivities.

The marriage ceremony, when performed in strict compliance with the rules, is a more complicated business for the Hindu than it is for his European brother. There are many forms for it, one of which is as follows:—

A sacred fire is prepared and west thereof a grinding-stone is placed, while to the north-east stands a jar of water, from the Ganges for preference. The bride squats close by, with her face towards the east, and the bridegroom advances towards her; if he desires sons they hold one another by the thumbs, if daughters by the fingers, and, if both, he holds the back of her hands with his thumbs—needless to say, fingers are seldom held. He then leads her three times round the fire and jar, repeating "I am he, thou art she; thou art she, I am he; I am the heaven, thou art the earth; I am the *Saman*, thou art the *Rik*. Come let us marry, let us possess offspring; united in affection, illustrious, well-disposed towards each other, let us live a hundred years."

Each time, after completing the circle, the bride stands upon the stone, while the bridegroom calls upon her to "be firm as her pedestal." The bride's mother pours *ghee* into her daughter's open hands and drops some rice into them; this mixture is thereupon thrown into the fire and a text recited.

The bridegroom next unties the two tresses of her hair, one on each side of the bride's head, and announces that she is "let loose from the fetters of Varuna." After this she takes seven steps towards the north-east for energy, strength, wealth, health, offspring, fair weather, and friendship. Further wishes having been expressed regarding devotion and the production of sons, water from the jar is sprinkled over both their heads brought close together.

The bridegroom should remain that night in the abode of an old Brahman woman, whose husband and children are alive.

When the bride sees the Polar star in conjunction with *Arundhati* (one of the Pleiades) and the seven *Rishis* (the seven stars of the Great Bear) she should bless her husband and pray for children.

The bridegroom should give away the bride's dress to one who knows the *Surya Sukta* (Rig-Veda X, 85).

The ceremonies close with a feast to the Brahmans.

A marriage seldom takes place among Hindus during the four months of the rainy season, for during that period the Great Preserver is down on a visit to Raja Bali and cannot therefore bless the contract with his divine presence.

In some parts of India curious customs exist of marrying two trees, or a stone to a tree or bush. *Salagrams*, or stones containing fossil impressions of ammonites and considered to be representations of Vishnu, are sometimes married to the ***tulasi*** (Ocymum sanctum), a small sacred shrub ; the stone will be taken in procession to the shrub and all the ceremonies of an ordinary marriage performed.

The legend of the Nerbudda river is quaint, and shows how inanimate objects are sometimes regarded as living beings :—

The River Son, which rises near the source of the Nerbudda not far from Amarkantak, flows west for some miles and then, suddenly turning to the east, is joined by a small stream called the Johila, before it falls over a great cascade.

The legend runs that the Son was betrothed to Miss Nerbudda and was proceeding with a ***barat*** (marriage procession) to fetch his bride ; she was curious to see what he was like and sent little Miss Johila to spy. Son met this young lady and fell in love with her ; so Miss Nerbudda got in a furious temper, threw rocks about and, with a terrific kick, sent them bounding over the precipice towards the east, while she proceeded in the opposite direction.

The Nerbudda, like most of the other rivers in India, is a deity, and in one of her temples there is a statue of Miss Johila bound in chains.

Death Ceremonies.—The funeral rites of Hindus vary considerably, but it is an almost invariable practice to cremate the corpse and to throw the ashes, or a portion of them, into the Ganges or some other sacred river. If the relatives are wealthy they spend a great deal over costly fuel, lengthy ceremonies, feasts and gifts to the Brahmans, but, if poor, a few rupees will cover the expenses.

According to the Shastras the burning ground should be selected at a spot which should be south-east or south-west of the deceased's residence. After the hair and nails have been clipped off, the corpse is carried here on a litter in procession; the nearest relations follow in single file, oldest behind and the men separated from the women; the other mourners, eldest first and youngest after, bring up the rear, with their sacrificial cords and clothes hanging down and their hair dishevelled.

On arrival at the spot the leader of the ceremony sprinkles the body with holy water and repeats Rig-Veda X, 14,9: "Depart (ye evil spirits) slink away from here; the Fathers (ancestors) have made for him this place of rest, distinguished by days (*ahobhir*), waters (*adbhir*), and bright lights (*aktubhih*)."

The logs for the fire are piled up and on the top a layer of sweet-scented grass is spread, the whole being kept in position by iron stakes. A goat is now killed and skinned, and the corpse, covered with a fine white cloth, is carried thrice round the funeral pile and finally deposited on it, together with the clipped hair and nails, the skin of the goat, and various other articles. Holy water is sprinkled and texts repeated.

At this stage the widow advances, with her husband's sword if he was a soldier, and lies down by the logs. Her brother-in-law, or an old servant, thereupon summons her to arise by repeating Rig-Veda X, 18,8 : " Rise O woman, return to the world of life, thou art reclining by a corpse. Thou hast fulfilled thy duties to the husband who married thee and led thee by the hand." The same person removes the sword and gives instructions for the fires to be lighted. This is done in three different places at the same time; to the south-east is the *Ahavaniya* fire, which sends the dead man's spirit to heaven if it reaches first; to the north-west is *Garhapatya*, which conveys it to the middle region; and south-west is *Dakshina*, which keeps it in the world of mortals.

When the fire has burnt itself out the leader of the ceremonies repeats Rig-Veda X, 18,3 : " We living men, survivors, now return and leave the dead; may our oblations please the gods and bring us blessings; now we go to dance and jest and hope for longer life."

The funeral party then proceed to bathe and, on coming out of the water, put on fresh clothes. They should not return to their homes until the sun has set, and before entering their houses should purify themselves by touching fire, a stone, cow-dung, barley, oil, and water. There are special rules as to what food they are to eat during the next few days.

After the tenth day of the dark half of the month, and on an odd day the ashes are gathered and placed in a vase, which is covered with a lid and buried in the earth. When this has been done the relations return home and, after washing, offer a *sraddha*, or offering to the deceased. Brahmans are then feasted and gifts are presented to them.

These are the rites laid down in the *Smarta Shastra*, but nowadays the favoured place for the cremation ceremony is the bank of a sacred river; the ashes are consigned to the waters and not as a rule buried in the earth. It is also a practice for one of the relations to fracture the skull of the deceased during the burning in order to facilitate the escape of the spirit. Gosains, however, do not cremate, but bury their dead.

The practice of *suttee* does not appear to have been directed in any of the ancient Shastras; in Rig-Veda X, 18,3, it is distinctly ordered that the widow is to come back from the funeral pile, and there is nothing in the Veda to authorize the burning of the widow with her deceased husband. It seems to be the remnant of a Scythian custom which has mostly been followed by races of Tartar origin.

CHAPTER VII.

HINDU GODS OF TO-DAY.

IT is not an exaggeration to state that there are many millions of gods and goddesses in the Hindu pantheon, and yet there are not millions of gods, but one God ; for, if we question an ordinary Hindu about any matter regarding which he desires to express ignorance, his reply will be *Khuda janta*, 'God knows'; or, if we speak to a Hindu ascetic, as likely as not we shall receive no answer in words, but, instead, he will point one finger upwards towards the heavens, as though to imply that he cannot be interrupted while he is meditating upon the "One God."

It has already been mentioned that the Aryans seem to have believed originally in one God, but that this deity was gradually split up into a number of others. We have seen that, in the course of time, the names of the principal gods were altered and a triumvirate, or trinity, was formed ; also that there were numerous offshoots from the members of this trinity. To these were added myriads of minor deities, including good and evil spirits, demons and fairies, objects animate and inanimate ; many of which were borrowed from the pre-Aryan beliefs. New deities also took shape from ideas put forward by philosophers. All of these new gods, combined with many of the old ones in their original or in corrupted shapes, form the amazing mass of Hindu mythology of the present day.

The *Trimurti*, or trinity, consists of *Brahmā*, the 'Creator'; *Vishnu*, the 'Preserver'; and *Siva*, the 'Destroyer'; these three being manifestations of *Brahmă* the all-pervading 'Divine Essence.'

Brahma generally appears as a red or orange-coloured figure with four heads. Some say that he once possessed five, but one was cut off by Siva because he would not acknowledge his superiority as Vishnu had done; others declare that this punishment was inflicted upon him because of his attempt to seduce his daughter Sarasvati, the goddess of learning, whom he eventually married. He has also four arms, in one of which he holds a spoon, in another a string of beads, in the third a water-vessel, and in the fourth the Veda. He is frequently attended by his *vahan*, or 'vehicle,' the *hansa*, or 'goose.'

Brahmā is not one of the popular gods and there are few temples specially dedicated to him, but he is particularly reverenced at Pakher in Ajmer and at Bithur in the Doab, where at the Brahmavarta Ghat there is a large annual *mela* (fair); his images are, however, sometimes placed in the temples of other gods and worshipped with them.

Sarasvati is the wife, or *sakhti* (female energy), of Brahmā and is analogous in Western mythology to Minerva, the patroness of learning. She is the goddess of music, poetry, learning, and eloquence, indeed of all the arts and sciences. The fifth of Magh is her special day, and she is then worshipped with offerings of perfumes, flowers, and dressed rice ; implements of writing and books being reverenced and presented. She is also propitiated in marriage ceremonies. The goddess is sometimes depicted as a white woman standing on a lotus, holding a lute in her hand · at others, riding upon a peacock and carrying the same emblem.

Vishnu is the second person in the triad and is worshipped as the Supreme Being by a vast number of Hindus, his worshippers being called Vaishnavas. His nine *ăvătars* (incarnations) have already been described ; of these Rama and Krishna are the only ones of importance nowadays. He is also called Rama and Narayan, but is best known to the general public under his name Jagganath, or 'Lord of the World' ; as such he is worshipped at Puri in Orissa and his car festival (described in Chapter X) there is world-famous.

Vishnu is a personification of the preserving power, and the sun is supposed to be a type of him ; he is, however, sometimes the earth and also water, or humidity generally, likewise air and space.

In pictures Vishnu's ethereal character is indicated by mounting him on a *garuda,* a creature half eagle and half man ; he is also shown in the shape of any of his incarnations and his pictures may generally be distinguished from those of other deities by the accompanying shell and the disc called *chakra* His *ăvătars* usually carry a mace and a lotus.

Vishnu, regarded as time, corresponds with the Florus of Egypt. The legends of his sleeping, awaking, and turning on his side, evidently allude to the sun at the solstices; also to the phenomena of the overflow and receding of the Ganges, so similar to that of the Nile in Egypt. He is fabled to arise from his slumber of four months on the 11th or the 14th of the bright half of the lunar month Kartik. When this period is half over he is supposed to turn himself on his side on the 11th of Bhadra.

Vishnu is represented of a black or blue colour; he possesses four arms and holds a club with which to punish the wicked; the *chonk*, or shell, is for sounding on joyful occasions; the whirling *chakra* shows his universal domination; and the *lotus*, or water lily, typifies his creative power. The *chakra*, or discus, resembles a wheel or quoit, a sort of missile weapon whirled round the middle finger and used as a weapon of war. Sometimes he is seated on a throne composed of the sacred lotus, with his favourite wife, Lakshmi, in his arms; or standing between her and his other wife, Satyavama, on a lotus; at others he reclines on a lotus leaf or on the serpent, *ananta* (eternity), floating on the water; or he rides on his *vahan* (vehicle) *garuda*.

No sanguinary sacrifices are offered to him, and he is regarded as a household and peaceful god.

Lakshmi is goddess of beauty, love, prosperity, intellect, and speech; she is spoken of as omnipresent, the eternal mother of the universe. It is said that she issued from the ocean of milk, when it was churned by the demons and gods; thereupon she was crowned and, being adorned with heavenly jewels and a wreath of everlasting flowers, was received in the arms of Vishnu as his bride. She became incarnate in Sita, the chaste and beautiful wife of Rama, and in Rukmini and Radha, the wife and favourite mistress, respectively, of Krishna. Radha is considered a lucky name for women, and such names as Radha Krishna, Lakshmi Narain, Ram Narain, Ram Chand, Bishan (Vishan) Chand, and Jagganath are common among men.

The principal festivals, in which Vishnu, his incarnations, or his wives are worshipped, are Anant Chaudash, Janam-Ashtami (Krishna's birth-day), Dussehra and Ram Lila (Rama's victory), Diwali and Basant Panchmi.

Siva, Shiva, or **Mahadeo**, is the third god of the Hindu triad and is worshipped by the Saiva sect, who form the greater number of Hindus. Magnificent temples have been erected throughout India in his honour, and in almost every village may be seen the small shrine called a *Shivala*, which is built for his propitiation and worship, usually by a *bunia*, or 'grain merchant.' These buildings invariably contain the *linga*, the creative emblem of Siva, in the shape of a rounded stone or lump of clay, surrounded sometimes by a circular ridge of clay to represent the female symbol *yoni*; outside one of these small shrines there often appears the image of a bull (*Nanda*), which is sacred to this god in his constructive capacity.

Siva is known by a large variety of names, among which is Chiun, a god mentioned in the Book of Amos (Chap. V. 25, 26). His attributes are many. As the destroyer he is named Isa or Isvara, Rudra, Hara Sambhu, Mahadeva or Mahesha. He is also Fire and the Sun, the destroyer and generator.

As the deity presiding over generation his emblem is the *linga,* like the *phallus* of Egypt, Greece, and Rome. He usually carries a *trisula* (trident) to represent the trinity. He is depicted as of white colour, with reddish hair, and possessing two, four, eight, or ten hands and five faces. This god and his *ăvătars* have a third eye on the forehead, with the corners up and down, and he is commonly shown bedecked with serpents as emblems of eternity and wearing a necklace of human heads to mark his character of destruction.

The *linga* is never carried in procession, but small clay models of it are made on the banks of the Ganges and thrown into the river after worship. Images of Siva in his many other forms are conveyed through the streets of Calcutta and other places after the festivals in his honour and cast into the river.

Kali.—Siva's wife *Kali,* as goddess of destruction and darkness, is truly awful in her actions, being responsible for almost every evil under the sun; but as Durga she appears in her creative form and is a more pleasant deity. She has a variety of names, such as Parvati, Devi, Bhairavi, and Uma.

Kali is usually shown as of black or dark blue colour, trampling on the body of Siva ; in one hand she holds a blood-stained sword and in the other a gory human head ; a third hand points downwards to destruction and the fourth is raised in allusion to a new creation. She wears a necklace of human heads, and her portrait can be immediately recognised by its awfulness.

Durga, whose emblem is the *yoni*, has ten arms ; in one hand is a spear with which she is piercing the giant Muhesha, in another a sword ; in a third the hair of the giant and the tail of a serpent which is twined round him, and in others, a trident, discus, axe, club, arrow, and a shield. One of her feet presses on the body of the giant and the other rests on the back of a lion which is biting the giant's arm. She wears a magnificent crown and richly jewelled dress. The giant is issuing from the body of the buffalo, into which he had transformed himself during the combat. In this busy position is the goddess represented at the *Durga Puja*, accompanied by her two sons Ganesha and Skanda and others.

Ganesha, the son of Siva and Durga, is the god of prudence and policy and the patron of letters. Although there are very few edifices specially dedicated to him, his image, in the shape of a short, fat, red-coloured man with a large belly and the head of an elephant, is to be found in most temples. He is invoked by many Hindus on the commencement of a business, the building of a house, or the beginning of a journey; the words *Sri Ganesh* will be found written on the flyleaf of many an account-book and often at the head of bankers' letters; his image, painted or sculptured, is frequently to be seen in, or over, the shops of bankers and others, and over the doorways of dwelling-houses; one of the gates of a Hindu city is generally named after him; indeed there is no other god of the Hindu pantheon who is so frequently seen and addressed.

Ganesha is often accompanied by a rat, and is sometimes shown riding upon one of these animals, which are regarded by Hindus as sagacious and prudent. It is this unfortunate fact which preserves the rat from destruction. This god generally has four arms, but occasionally six or eight, or perhaps only two; when there are four, one holds the *ankas*, or hook for guiding the elephant, another a shell, in the third is a conical ball, and in the fourth a vessel containing small cakes. Besides being inelegant in figure he is also a poor equestrian, and the story goes that, on one occasion, when he fell off his steed, the Moon, who was looking on, fell alaughing; Ganesha lost his temper and placed a curse upon her and upon all who should gaze upon her thereafter; luckily he was persuaded to modify this, and now it applies only to those who happen to glance at her on their birthdays.

Skanda, also known as Kartikeya, is the second son of Siva. He is the god of war and is regarded by thieves as their patron! He is variously depicted as possessing one or six faces ; two, four, or six arms, each of which holds a warlike instrument. His mother Parvati gave him a peacock which is the *vahan* of this warlike divinity.

Yama, in Hindu mythology, is the king of death and hell and *Pitripati*, or 'Lord of the Ancestors.' He is described as of a green colour, with red garments, having a crown on his head, his eyes inflamed, and sitting on a buffalo, with a huge club and *pash* (a cord or rope with which to strangle sinners) in his hands. His countenance, as seen by the virtuous, is divine ; but the wicked, when judged by him, see nothing but terror.

Yama is the *Sraddha-deva*, or 'Lord of Obsequies'. At the time of offering oblation to the *manes* (spirits) of deceased ancestors, he is invoked by the priest under numerous names, such as Dharma Rajah (king of the deities), Antaka (the destroyer), Kala (time). Daily offerings of water are made to Yama and the second day of the month of Kartik is sacred to him and his sister, the river goddess Yamana (Jumna), who then entertained him. In consequence of this, sisters make presents and offer delicacies to their brothers on that day. He is also worshipped on the 14th day of Asvin.

Sraddha is the ceremonial oblation in honour of deceased ancestors and is considered of great importance by most Hindus.

Yama Danshtra (Yama's teeth), which implies the last eight days of Asvin and the whole of Kartik, is considered to be a period of universal sickness, and the jaws of death are believed to be open during that time. Certainly the death-rate in India is generally highest then. Brahmans are particularly energetic in reading the Veda at that season, so that their souls may be prepared in case of a sudden call.

Kama or *Kandarp*, the son of Maya, or the general attracting power, is the god of love and corresponds to Cupid. He was married to Rati, or 'Affection,' and his bosom friend was Vasantha, or 'Spring.' He is represented as a beautiful youth riding by moonlight on a parrot, with an attendant bevy of nymphs, one of whom carries his standard, on which is depicted a fish on a red ground. This banner may sometimes be seen in wedding processions. His bow is made of sugarcane or flowers, the string is formed of bees, and his five arrows are pointed with strong-scented blossoms.

It was Kama who, when scarcely created, inspired Brahmā with a passion for his own daughter Sarasvati ; but when he amused himself by shooting an arrow at Siva, who was engaged at the time in austerities, this god became so enraged that he glanced at him with his third eye and thereby reduced him to ashes.

Prithvi, goddess of the Earth, is by some considered a form of Lakshmi, by others of Parvati. Daily offerings are made to her. The word means "conspicuous," so called because the Lord of Creation moulded it.

Hindus refer to the Earth, or Prithvi, as an example of patience or forbearance, permitting her bowels to be ripped open, her surface lacerated, and suffering every indignity without resentment or murmuring. She is also quoted as a model of righteousness in that she returns good for evil.

Prithvi is also called Bhu Devi, Bhuma Devi, and in Northern India is known by the name Dharta Mata. Most Hindus salute her when they arise in the morning and call on her for protection; agriculturists invoke her before ploughing and sowing; when a row is bought, or first calves, five streams of milk are allowed to fall upon the earth, as an offering, before any is taken, and the first stream is always so disposed of whenever a cow is milked; before medicine is taken, a little is sprinkled upon the ground in her honour.

Jawala-mukhi, or the 'Flames Mouth,' is a temple of the goddess of that name situate in the Kangra district in the valley of the Beas. It is built over some fissures in the sandstone rock from which issue natural jets of combustible gas, believed by the pilgrims to be a manifestation of the goddess Devi. It is also related that the flames proceed from the mouth of a demon-king named Jalandhara, whom Siva overwhelmed with mountains and after whom the Jalandhar (Jullundur) Doab is named. The Bhojki priests, who are the custodians of the temple, encourage the flames with libations of ghee, and they obtain a considerable income from the offerings made by the pilgrims in cash and kind.

Sendu Bir, or the 'Whistling Spirit,' is a godling to whom shrines are erected in Jammu, Kangra, and Gurdaspur. He is much feared by Hindu cultivators, who believe that he steals their corn and belongings to give to those who worship him, that he burns the houses of those with whom he is displeased, and that he has the power of cohabiting, while they are dreaming, with any women to whom he may be sent by persons who have acquired mystic charm from him. He is said to have the appearance of a shepherd, and when his whistling is heard it is desirable to make copious offerings for his propitiation and to provide a ram as his steed.

Narsingh, or *Anar Singh*, is another godling of some notoriety in the Kangra district. He is supposed to be an incarnation of Vishnu, and is somewhat mixed up with Krishna; people believe him to be empowered to give sons to barren women and to tide them over difficulties. Women are his chief adorers, and many of them keep a cocoanut as his emblem; on this they make a *tilak* out of sandal-wood paste and to it they pay respect, generally on a Sunday, by decorating it with flowers and burning incense. Narsingh is also believed to cohabit with his female worshippers during their dreams.

Guga Sheds. In many parts of Kangra may be seen little sheds containing images, among which the chief is one of a mounted deity named Guga. These idols are supposed to have the power of curing snake-bite. The Brahmans who officiate at these shrines are careful to declare that the god has been seriously offended in some manner, when they perceive that a patient is beyond recovery.

Amman is a goddess much worshipped by villagers in the south of India, who understand the word to mean 'mother'; she is described as Ankal or 'golden,' Kani, and Mutial or 'pearl,' Paleri or 'great.' The Mahrattas know her by the term *Ai*, or 'mother.' Sacrifices of sheep, goats and fowls, cocoanuts, fruit, ghee, and other things are made to her. The *pujari*, or officiating priest, is generally of the Sudra caste.

Hanuman, the monkey-god, is a favourite in the central part of India, where many temples are dedicated to him, sometimes in company with his companions Rama and Sita. He is supplicated by Hindus on their birthdays, for he is supposed to have power to bestow longevity.

Varuna, the great deity of Vedic days, has now become the god of waters; while *Indra* has greatly declined in power and only pays periodical visits to the earth.

Khwajr Khizr, the patron saint of the *bhestis*, or water-carriers of India, is really of Musalman origin, but is regarded as "god of water" by Hindus. His principal shrine is at Sonepat near Delhi.

Sacred Rivers. The Ganges, Jumna, Nerbudda, Godaveri, and many other rivers and streams are worshipped as deities and so are many other inanimate objects.

The *Ganges* is the goddess "*Ganga*" of Hindu mythology. The Saivas place her source in Siva's hair, but the Vaishnavas assert that she flowed from the foot of Krishna and fell on the head of Siva, who shook some drops from his hair and thus formed the great lake Bindu (drops) Sarovara. Some allege that the river issued from a cow's mouth and the gorge in the Himalayas, through which it flows, is called Gao-mukhi (cow-mouth) and Gangotri.

One of the holiest parts of the Ganges is where it joins the Jumna near Allahabad, and here annually occurs the *Magh Mela* (the Fair of Magh), the largest religious fair in India.

The *Ganga* is described as a white woman with a crown on her head, a water-lily in one hand, and a water-vessel in another; she rides upon a *vahan*, which resembles a crocodile, or walks upon the surface of the water with a lotus in each hand.

Stone worship exists to a large extent in many parts of India. In Southern India five stones, daubed with red and called the *Pandu*, are regarded as guardians of the fields. Ammonites and meteortes are worshipped as representatives of Vishnu.

There are many trees, shrubs, and plants which are either sacred to the gods, or are deities in themselves; indeed almost every prominent object —in the heavens above, in the earth beneath, or in the waters under the earth—is considered worthy of worship.

The Cow. Among living creatures, the cow is the most sacred and has long been so regarded. The

Aryan wanderers in Central Asia must have regarded her with veneration, but, when they took to agriculture in their Indian settlements, cattle became of the greatest importance to them; for the cow supplied food and drink, while bullocks pulled their carts and ploughs, drew up water from the wells, and trod out or threshed the corn; cattle-dung was likewise found useful, not only as manure, but also as fuel and for plastering the walls, floors, and roofs of houses. The bull was considered to be an emblem of creation.

All these points in favour of the cow and bull still hold good; indeed every part of a cow is pronounced to be holy, and it is a fact that the eating of the five products, including even its excreta, is regarded as a special means of purification.

Every morning a woman in the household smears the floors with cowdung mixed with water, partly as a holy duty and partly for cleanliness. She sprinkles the urine of the cow over her head and about the house in purification, whenever anything has occurred to make it, in their religion, unclean.

Every morning, on rising, a Hindu should, if possible, glance at a cow, a mirror, the sun, a rich man, a king, a priest, a charitable person, and a chaste woman. It is not, however, the cow's face but its tail, on which they cast their look, for there is no merit in its face.

When a Hindu is dying, his relations sometimes give a cow to a Brahman and repeat the gift on the eleventh day after the demise. On the occasion of a Brahman's marriage the bride's father is always expected to present a cow. Every Friday the cow should be washed, and it is frequently ornamented with *tilaks*.

Among other creatures, which receive respect and often worship, may be mentioned the monkey, celebrated in the Ramayana ; the fish, tortoise, and boar, as incarnations of Vishnu ; the wagtail, owing to emblematic marks on its throat, and the peacock ; the snake and the conch shell.

There is a whole series of *singha*, or 'snake gods and goddesses,' which are regarded as descendants of a king of Patal, and it is believed by many that the spirits of the dead sometimes enter snakes and do a lot of harm. Shrines are built to them, offerings of milk made, and prayers said, particularly on Sundays and at weddings.

Sitala, or *Mata*, goddess of smallpox, is the chief of a group of seven sisters, who cause pustulous diseases and have to be propitiated regularly by women and children ; the names of the other six are Agwāni, Basănti, Lamkāria, Mahāi Mai, Măsāni, and Polamdi. Small shrines are built for them in the villages, and the 7th day of Jeth, called Sili-satan or 'Sitala's seventh,' is fixed for special worship. If an infant dies of smallpox, the next born will be given some objectionable name such as *Kurria* (he of the dung-hill) to frighten these goddesses away. The day after the Holi festival is an auspicious occasion for ceremonies in honour of Sitala ; she is then placed upon a potter's donkey, which is led in procession to the shrine, where grain is waved over the head of a child and thereafter given to the donkey and its master.

Among local gods in the east of the Punjab, *Bhumia*, 'god of the homestead,' probably holds the chief position. He has a small shrine (*khera*) erected in his honour when a new village is built. Here the women and children say prayers on a Sunday; here Brahmans are fed on the occasion of domestic events and at harvest-time; and here oaths or statements made are considered as absolutely binding.

The women have to beware of *Gandarvas*, a kind of genii, who are fond of and dangerous to them.

The Mystic Hand. A common sign, used by people of various denominations in India, is that of the outstretched hand. It is called by Hindus the *abhāya hasta* (protecting hand) or *varāda hasta* (beneficent hand) and may be seen stamped upon the walls of temples and houses to protect the inmates against ill-luck, on bullocks to preserve them from disease, on sacred trees worshipped by women, and on the wall of a room in which a maiden's maturity ceremony takes place. It is usual for a person to smear *kunkuma* on his hand and imprint the mark on the walls of a freshly constructed building, both inside and out, or on the walls of a temple when a new idol is installed, and on clothes at weddings. The colours used are usually red or yellow.

The Swastica is a peculiar symbol or mystic cross, used especially in Tibet by a sect of that name but also throughout India by Hindus. The word is derived from *su* (well) and *asti* (it is), meaning "it is well" or "so be it" and implying complete resignation under all circumstances. This symbol was used by the Greeks in designs on their pottery, and it is commonly worn in Europe as a charm in the shape of a pendant.

The Crescent is worn as a sign by the god Siva and his consort Parvati, but it is extensively used by Muslims on their banners and is the well-known emblem of Turkey.

The following list is taken from "**Prinsep's Useful Tables**" published in 1834.

1. The Infinite Almighty Creator, of the Vedas, Brahm—

The Hindu Trinity, or Trimurti:	Brahmā,	Vishnu, ..	Siva.
Their consorts:	Saraswati, Sakti or Maya.	Lakshmi, .. Padma or Sri,	Parvati. Bhawani or Durga.
Their attributes:	Creator,	Preserver, ..	Destroyer.
Their attendant *vahan* or vehicle:	Hansa (goose),	Garuda (bird),	Nandi (bull).
Their symbols:	Time, Air,	Water, ..	Fire.
Their stations:	Meru,	The Sun, ..	Jupiter.
Their common titles, A.U.M.	Parameswara,	Narayana, ..	Mahadeva.
Figure under which worshipped:	Mentally,	Saligram and 9 *avataras*,	The *lingam*, under his million epithets.
Analogues in Western mythology:	Saturn,	Jupiter, ..	Jupiter.

2. Other members of the Hindu pantheon, and their supposed analogues in Western mythology, according to Sir Wm. Jones.

Saraswati ..	Minerva, patroness of learning.
Ganesha ..	Janus, god of wisdom.
Indra	Jupiter, god of firmament.
Varuna	Neptune, god of water.
Prithvi	Cybele, goddess of earth.
Viswakarma ..	Vulcan, architect of gods.
Kartikeya or Skanda	Mars, god of war.
Kama	Cupid, god of love.
Surya or Arka ..	Sol, the sun Mithra, the same.
Hanuman, son of Pavana	Pan, the monkey-god.
Rama	Bacchus, god of wine.
Yama	Pluto or Minos.
Heracula	Hercules.
Aswiculapa ..	Aesculapius (genii).
Vaitarini	The river Styx.
Durga	Juno.
Nareda	Mercury, music.
Krishna	Apollo.
Bhawani	Venus.
Kali or Durga ..	Proserpine.
Agni	Vulcan, fire.
Swaha	Vesta (his wife).
Aswini-kumara ..	Castor and Pollux.
Aruna	Aurora.
'Atavi Devi ..	Diana.
Kuvera	Plutus, god of riches.
Ganga	The river Ganges.
Vayu	Aeolus.
Sri	Ceres.
Anna Purna ..	Anna Perenna.

CHAPTER VIII.

HINDU FESTIVALS. (PART I.)

IN ancient days the Vedic poets had considerable knowledge of astronomy, but the study of this science, although continued by the Brahmans for a long period, began to decline when the Musalman incursions commenced about 1000 A.D., and nowadays Hindu astronomers are few and far between.

The dates for Hindu festivals were invariably fixed in accordance with the position of various heavenly bodies at the time of events which led to them; in this chapter, therefore, reference will be made to the luni-solar months in which the festivals occur and a few words regarding the Hindu Calendar will not be out of place.

To begin with, it may be mentioned that Hindus consider that there are four lengthy *Yuga*, or 'Ages' of time, namely :—

1st. *Krita* or *Satya*, the 'Golden Age' or that of 'Truth,' which extends for a period of 1,728,000 years and is in four parts.

2nd. The *Treta Yuga*, which lasts for 1,296,000 years. It has three (*treta*) parts and is known as the 'Silver Age.'

3rd. That of *Dwapara* (two parts), extending for 864,000 years.

4th. The *Kali Yuga* or present 'Evil Age,' which has a period of 432,000 years (one part).

According to Bentley, who worked them out on astronomical data, these Ages commenced on the 19th April 2352, 28th October 1528, 15th September 901, and 8th February 540 B.C., respectively.

The usual system of reckoning dates is that of the Samvat Era, founded in 57 B.C. by a king named Vikramaditya Sakari to commemorate his victories over the Scythians. Another is the Saka Era which began in 78 A.D., and was in honour of another king called Salivahana, who likewise fought against these invaders.

The names of the months were taken from the *nakshatras*, or 'asterisms,' in which the moon was supposed to be full at different times of the year. In some parts of India the Hindu Calendar commences with the month Vaisakh, but in Northern India it begins with Chait.

It is, however, convenient to follow the more ancient divisions of time in describing the principal Hindu festivals; that is, when the year opened with Magh and the spring festivities, and closed with the winter solstice in the month of Poh.

The Hindu divides the year into six seasons, each of two months, namely—*Vasanta* (Spring), *Greeshma* (Summer), *Varsha* (Rainy), *Sarad* (Sultry), *Hemanta* (Cold), and *Sisira* (Dewy).

The months and chief festivals are :—

SEASONS.	NAMES OF MONTHS.	ENGLISH EQUIVALENTS.	PRINCIPAL FESTIVALS.
Sisira	Magh, Magha	January—February	Makar Sankranti, Basant Panchami, Pongal, Mahadeo pilgrimage.
	Phagan, Phalgun	February—March	Sheoratri, Holi.
Vasanta	Chait, Chaitra, Kait	March—April	Rama-navami, Durga Ashtami, Rati-ka-mela.
	Baisakh, Vaisakha	April—May	Vaisakhi, Savitri-vrata.
Greeshma	Jeth, Jait, Chet, Jyaishtha	May—June	Apsaras, Aranaya-shashti.
	Asarh, Asad, Ashadha, Sarh.	June—July	Vishnu's descent to Patal, Rath-yatra.
Varsha	Sawan, Sravana	July—August	Amar Nath pilgrimage, Naga Panchami, Solono. Pracha Amavasya.
	Bhadon, Bhadrapada	August—September	Anant Chaudash, Janam Ashtami, Narali Paurnima, Ganesh Chaturthi.
Sarad	Kuar, Asoj, Asvina	September—October	Pitra Paksha, Dussehra, Ram Lila, Durga Puja.
	Kartik, Kartika	October—November	Bali Pratipada, Diwali.
Hemanta	Aghan, Margasirsha, Agrahayana.	November—December	Champa Shashti.
	Poh, Pusa, Paush	December—January.	

Lunar days are called *Tithi*, but the solar days of the week are called *Vara* or *Var* and are named after the following planets, by adding the affix *Var* like " day " :—

English.	*Hindi.*
Sun,	Aditya, Surya or Ravi.
Moon,	Soma.
Mars,	Mangala.
Mercury,	Budha.
Jupiter,	Brihaspati.
Venus,	Sukra.
Saturn,	Sani.

Each day of the week has a sacred significance—Aditya means the 'Great God,' Surya and Ravi mean the Sun. Monday is especially sacred to Siva, and is observed by some as a fast ; the *linga* being worshipped in the evening. Saturday is Hanuman's day ; it is regarded as unlucky, for Sani is believed to be a malignant god who requires propitiation. Thursday is the great day for worshipping ancestors ; in the evening lights twinkle at Muslim shrines and Hindu temples throughout India.

Some festivals and fairs are held at intervals longer than a year, the time being regulated by the position of certain celestial bodies ; thus great religious fairs (*mela*) take place at various holy centres, such as Kurukshetra (Thanesar) and Prayag (Allahabad), whenever there is an eclipse of the sun.

The Month of Magh.

Basant Panchami, or Makar Sankranti. *Basant* or *Vasant*, means 'Spring,' and *Makara* is the equivalent of Capricorn. When the Sun is in the sign of Makara on the 5th of the bright half of Magh, Jagaddhatri, goddess of Spring and nourisher of the world, is worshipped. The sign of Makara—a creature with the head and forelegs of an antelope and body and tail of a fish—is the emblem of Kandarp, or Kama, the god of love, who likewise receives adoration on this occasion, along with his spouse Rati, the goddess of love, and Lakshmi.

The *Vasant Rag*, or 'Spring Song,' is sung and its special virtue is said to be the giving of an impulse to the emotions of love and merriment.

Food is coloured with saffron, and yellow clothes are worn to represent the appearance of the Spring crops, also a nautch is considered seasonable.

In some places the cattle have their horns painted and decorated, and they are given a well-earned holiday.

The sun is said to begin his journey northward by entering Capricorn, so he is worshipped, and there are enormous gatherings to bathe at Prayag (Allahabad), where the Ganges and Jumna become united, and at Ganga Sagar, where the Ganges enters the bosom of the ocean (*sagar*); the former fair is well known by the name of *Magh Mela.*

Pongal. In Southern India a festival called *Pongal* (a Tamil word meaning "boiling") takes place at this time on the 1st day of the Tamil year. It is in honour of the birth of Mithras (the Sun) and the renewal of the solar year. There is much rejoicing because the unlucky month of Poh is over, and because each day of the ensuing month is regarded as lucky. For some time beforehand the people are warned by *sannyasis* to be careful and make offerings to Siva ; every morning the women clear little spaces before their houses and make lines thereon with flowers, over which they place small balls of cowdung, sticking into each a citron blossom. These are probably designed to represent Vighnesvara, eldest son of Isvara (Siva), the lord of the triad and remover of obstacles. Each day these little lumps of cowdung are collected with their flowers and carefully preserved until the last day of Poh, when, with much music and clapping of hands, the women march from their houses and dispose of the relics on some waste ground. On the following day begins the festival, the first day of which is called *Bhogi Pongal, i.e.* 'Indra's Pongal'. The second day is *Surya Pongal* in honour of the Sun. Married women bathe with their clothes on, and, on coming out of the water, set about boiling rice with milk. When it is ready they cry *Pongal* (boiling), and taking it off give some as an offering to an image of Vighnesvara and some to cows and then distribute the remainder. Other ceremonies are afterwards performed and they continue until the seventh day, but the second is the great day of the festival.

The Month of Phalgun.

Sheoratri, *Siva-Ratri*, or *Mahasiva Ratri*. This is a fast observed on the 14th day of the dark fortnight of *Phalgun* ; it means the 'Night of Siva' and the ceremonies take place chiefly at night. This fast is said to have been first observed by a powerful king named Chitra Bhanu of the Ikshvaku dynasty, who ruled over the whole of Jambu-Dwipa, another ancient name for India. On this day a celebrated deformed sage, Ashta Bakra, came to his court with some pupils and, finding him fasting, asked the reason. The king said that in his previous birth he had been a hunter and one day, when out searching for game, he shot a deer, but was overtaken by darkness and climbed into a *bel* tree for safety. While there he wept bitterly because his wife and children were without food and his tears fell, together with *bel* leaves, onto a *linga* at the foot of the tree. Siva imagined that these were offerings made to him. On the following morning the hunter returned, sold the deer, and bought food for his family. Just as they were commencing their meal a stranger arrived, and he was first fed according to custom. The hunter lived for many years without learning that he had by chance fasted on the day of Siva-Ratri, but when the hour of death drew near two messengers from Siva appeared to conduct his soul to paradise, and he then learnt that he was being rewarded for having observed the fast on that auspicious day and night. His soul remained in various heavens until it reached the highest, and he was afterwards reborn in high rank as a king and was specially favoured by being given the knowledge of his former life.

Pious Hindus abstain from food and drink during the day, and at night worship the god Siva by dropping water with *bel* leaves onto the emblem of Siva. The telling of the story of the hunter during the night is believed to give much merit to the listeners.

To please the god especially, the night should be divided into four *pahars*, or quarters, of three hours each ; at the end of each *pahar* a bath should be taken in milk, curd, *ghee*, and honey, respectively, followed by a service which may include singing and dancing. Fast and vigilance on this night, coupled with the baths and services, are said to give happiness in this and the next world, even to an outcaste.

Before breaking the fast in the morning Brahmans should be fed in memory of the stranger and the following prayer should be said : "Oh Shankar (Peace-Giver) Siva ! My beautiful Lord, be propitiated with this my fast, which has the effect of burning the ties of this world. Grant me the eye of knowledge."

Benares is a stronghold of Siva worship, and there the fast and other rites are performed with great solemnity.

Holi. The *Holi* is a popular festival celebrated during the ten days preceding the full moon of *Phalgun*.

The name is a corruption of the Sanskrit word *Holaka*, meaning 'half-ripe corn,' and seems to have originally been the *Vasant-utsava*, or Spring festival, when ceremonies were performed in honour of the crops and to ward off disease from the fields. Even now there is a remnant of these in the eating of stalks of half-ripe wheat and barley and in the burning of cakes of cowdung. The main festival, however, has developed into something quite different and has become the Saturnalia of India.

There is a legend that a terrible female demon, named Holaka, was accustomed to make her daily meal of children. The people appealed to a certain demon-king, who directed that the fury was to limit her appetite and only devour one child a day, also that the people might draw lots as to which it should be. One day the only grandson of a lonely old woman was selected in this manner for sacrifice on the following morning. Bemoaning his fate she was wandering about, when she encountered a *sadhu*, who declared that if Holaka were met with sufficiently strong abuse and foul language she would be subjugated. The old woman spread the news abroad and early next morning collected all the children, who had been instructed what to say, and, when Holaka appeared, they all greeted her with such a torrent of abuse and obscene expressions that she fell dead on the spot and the children made a huge bonfire of her remains.

The festival of the present day is in celebration of this event, and has become the occasion of licentious joy, drunkenness, evil singing, and dancing. Many persons lose all sense of respect for age, sex, and religion—the foulest language is used, clothes are smeared with red powder (*kunkuma*) mixed with water, and this is squirted over every one indiscriminately. Respectable women have to keep at home or meet with insults and obscene jokes. When the bonfire is lighted, however, some of them venture out to hold their infants near the flames for a few moments, as this is believed to act as a charm against evil influences.

It is probably something more than a coincidence that the Roman festival of *Anna Perenna* was celebrated at this time of the year and was somewhat similar to that of the *Holi.*

Phulguni, the goddess of Spring, is analogous with the "Phagesia" of the Greeks, and the word is compounded of *phala*, 'fruit' or 'fructifier,' and *guna*, 'quality.' *Phula* and *phala*, 'flower' and 'fruit,' are the roots of *Floralia* and *Phalasa*, the Phallus of Osiris (*lingam* of Isvara).

The month of Phalgun is celebrated in Rajputana with great éclat. It commences with the *Ahairea*, or great Spring-Hunt and, as success on this occasion in slaying the boar in honour of Gouri, the Ceres of the Rajputs, means good luck for the future, the competition is extreme.

As Phalgun advances there is much Bacchanalian mirth, and this is the time when red powder is scattered about, or a solution squirted at one another and passers-by. The festival of *Holi* commences about the full moon at the approach of the vernal equinox, and this season is peculiarly dedicated to Krishna; images of this deity are carried in procession with much music and singing; nautches and feasts are provided by the wealthy.

The Month of Chait.

Rama-navami. *Rama-navami*, the birthday of Rama, is observed on the 9th of the light half of the month of Chait and is kept by some as a strict fast. The temples of Rama are illuminated and his image is adorned; the Ramayana is read in the temples and there are nautches at night. In Rajputana horses and elephants and all the implements of war are worshipped on this day.

Rali Mela. The *Rali-ka-Mela* is a festival, or rather a series of festivals, which takes place throughout the month of Chait in the Kangra district. It is celebrated by young girls in memory of a maiden named *Rali*.

The legend is that a Brahman gave his grown-up daughter Rali in marriage to a child named Shankar. When she discovered her fate she stopped the bearers of her *dooly* by the side of a river and announced to her brother Bastu that she would live no more; she directed that, in future, girls should make clay images of herself and her husband, perform the marriage ceremony, and then convey them to the river in a *dooly*, and drown them there. Having spoken thus, she threw herself into the stream and was drowned, her example being promptly followed by Shankar and Bastu in their grief. During the month of Chait little girls take baskets of grass and flowers to certain spots for a period of about ten days, and, when a large heap has been collected, they cut a couple of large forked sticks, fix them—prongs downwards—over the heaps and on their pointed ends attach two clay images, one of Siva and the other of Parvati. All the ceremonies of a marriage are celebrated—the fetching of the bride with the *barat* (marriage procession), the actual marriage rites, and even the wedding feast at the conclusion.

Finally, on the 1st of Baisakh when the sad event is said to have occurred, the images are carried to the nearest stream and immersed amid much weeping and wailing. Girls, who join in this festival, expect to secure good husbands thereby. Considerable excitement is caused sometimes by small boys who dive and fish out the images in order to tease the girls.

Durga Ashtami. On the 8th of Chait in Rajputana there is a great festival of flowers in honour of Gouri (Parvati or Durga), wife of Isvara (or Siva), for this is the anniversary of her birthday. The meaning of Gouri is 'yellow,' emblematic of the ripened corn, and the ceremonies really form a kind of harvest festival. In other parts of India the festival in honour of Durga is held in the month of Asvin.

The Month of Baisakh.

Baisakhi, or *Vaisakhi*, also termed *Mekh Sankranti*, *Samvat-Saradi*, and *Vishnu Chaitraishu*. is the Hindu "New Year's Day" and falls on the date on which the Sun enters the sign Aries, either the latter part of Chait or early in Baisakh. Bathing in the Ganges and other sacred rivers is propitious. *Sattu* (meal of parched gram) and a water-pitcher should be given to Brahmans for the benefit of *pitra* or *manes* (deceased ancestors); shoes and umbrellas may likewise be bestowed. In order to divert any evil which the New Year may bring, it is necessary to take a bath in water, mixed with *dhatura* (datura fastuosa, or thorn apple) seeds and medicines, just at the time when the sun is entering Aries; the precise moment can be ascertained by floating two petals of a fresh rose in a basin of water, for they move towards one another and come into contact at the exact instant!

The day is not sacred to any special deity, but nevertheless pious Hindus visit the temples of their favourite gods, and in the evening the calendar of the new year is read out and expounded by Brahmans. Gala dress is worn and the day passed in merriment, but the company of women and the use of oil and meat should be eschewed. As a charm against snake-bite, *masur* (ervum lens, a pulse) and two *neem* leaves may be eaten.

On the Konkan or Malabar Coast in the Bombay Presidency there are great festivities on this day; gifts are presented by the heads of families to the various members, and all valuables are collected in the room devoted to the family god and there worshipped.

Savitri-vrata (Holy fig-tree). On the 29th of Baisakh there is a fast peculiar to women, who perform certain rites under the sacred fig-tree, the *vata* or *pipal*, to preserve them from widowhood.

The Month of Jeyt.

Apsaras. On the 2nd of Jeyt, when the Sun is in the zenith, Rajput ladies commemorate the birth of the sea-born goddess Rambha, the queen of the naiads, or *apsaras* (*ap*, 'water' and *sara*, 'froth'), whose birth, like that of Venus, was from the foam of the waters.

Aranya Shashti. *Aranya* (woods) *Shashti* (sixth) is a festival held by women in Rajputana on the 6th Jeyt. On this day those desirous of offspring walk in the woods to gather and eat certain herbs. Sir W. Jones remarked the analogy between this and the Druidic ceremony of gathering the mistletoe (also on the 6th day of the moon) as a preservative against sterility.

The Month of Asarh.

Jagannath. The *Ratha Yatra* (car procession), or procession of the Car of Jagannath or Vishnu (lord of the universe), occurs at Puri in Orissa on the 2nd and the 11th of Asarh, the "night of the gods," when Vishnu (the Sun) reposes for four months.

No less than sixty-two festivals are celebrated at this place during the year, but the principal is that of Jagannath's Car. The image of this god is a huge block of wood, with a hideous face and distended mouth; his arms are of gold and he is gorgeously clothed, as are the other two idols which accompany him in his temple at Puri.

In the festivals the images brought out are those of Krishna, his brother Bālarāma, and sister Subhadra.

The procession is also called *Padha Jatra*, and is in much repute with the Hindus of Bengal and Orissa.

Vishnu's descent *to Patal.* Vishnu is supposed to have descended to the world below (*Patal* or 'Hades') at the end of Asarh in order to protect Raja Bali from the attacks of Indra. He did not return until the latter part of Kartik, so during his absence all festivities and marriages were suspended, and it is now most unlucky to hold such ceremonies during this interval of four months (middle of July to the middle of November); there is always a rush of weddings just before and after that period.

CHAPTER IX.

HINDU FESTIVALS (PART II).

The Month of Sawan or Sravana.

THE Ṡun turns towards the south in the middle of the constellation Carcataca, over which the Serpents preside.

The third day of this month is sacred to Parvati, goddess of the Himalayas ; it is the day on which, after long austerities, she was reunited to Siva. She pronounced it holy and proclaimed that any one invoking her at this time would attain his desires ; the day is therefore much observed by women and it is an auspicious time at which to take possession of land, occupy a building, or start a business, and so on.

Naga Panchami (Serpent 5th day). The fifth day of this month is set apart for the propitiation of Naga, the chief of the reptile race, and indeed of all snakes. Offerings of milk, grain, and other articles are made, and if live snakes cannot be obtained these things are poured into the holes where they are likely to be. Early in the morning each family brings out a clay or wooden model of a snake or a painting of from five to nine. If there is a temple devoted to the Nagas in the vicinity, people go there to worship.

In the Kanara district in the south of India serpent-worship is much practised, and at many temples consecrated snakes are reared by the *pandarams* and fed daily at the expense of the worshippers; women especially perform ceremonies in their honour.

The Nagas, or serpent-genii of the Rajputs, have a semi-human structure.

There is a sculptured column in a cave temple in the south of India on which is a representation of the first human pair at the foot of a fruit tree and a serpent, entwined among the heavily laden boughs, is presenting to them some of the fruit from his mouth. There is a tradition of the Jains which asserts that the human species were created in pairs called *Joogal*, who fed of the ever-fructifying *Calpa-vriksha*, which possesses all the characteristics of the "Tree of Life."

On the occasion of the *Naga Panchami* plants are strewn about the threshold to prevent the entrance of reptiles, and they are regarded, by some, more as demons, who have to be propitiated, than as gods; indeed we read that Vishnu is attended by an eagle named Garuda which acts as a protector against them.

Pethuri, or *Pracha Amawasya.* This festival is held on the new moon of Sawan in honour of the 64 Yogini, or female attendants of the goddess Durga. It is chiefly observed by women who have lost infant children, but men also engage in the holiday and purchase sweetmeats and toys for children.

Solono. *Solono* is a festival performed in honour of the good genii, when Durvasa, the sage, instructed Salone (the genius or nymph presiding over the month of Sawan) to bind on Rakhis, or bracelets, as charms to avert evil. Brahmans and females alone are privileged to bestow these charmed wrist-bands. The occasion is also called *Rishi Tarpani*, 'the day on which to please the gods.' It takes place when the full moon falls on the Sravan constellation and is celebrated by the twice-born, more especially by Brahmans. On this occasion sisters and brothers exchange gifts.

The ceremony of *Rakhi* (*Raksha*) *Bandhan* consists in tying on the wrist a thread made of silk, cotton, and coloured cloth, mixed with gold thread and *akshat* (rice or flowers). It is tied on the wrist of a ruler by the *Raj-purohit* (royal priest) and on those of the public by Brahmans or women. The following text is recited during the rite :—" With which was tied King Bali, the lord of giants of great strength, with the same I tie you, be protected : Do not go, do not go."

Persons thus tied are considered to be safe during the succeeding year from snakes, ancestors' spirits, demons, and all other evils (see also *Anant Chaudash*).

The Month of Bhadon.

Janam Ashtami. *Janam Ashtami* means the '8th day of birth,' and commemorates the birth of Krishna, which is said to have occurred at midnight on the 8th Bhadon. A fast is observed during the whole day only to be broken the following morning. During the day Dwarki, the mother of Krishna, Vasudeva, his father, Nanda and Yashoda, his step-parents, and Baldeo, his elder brother, are all worshipped. Brahmans place a *salagram* (black stone) in a cucumber to represent the pregnant Dwarki, and at midnight ghee and *gur* are offered; the stone is then taken out and all ceremonies, observed on the birth of a child, are performed. After this the men and women break their fast by first sipping a mixture of milk, curd, and basil leaves. Clay images of the infant Krishna, swung in cradles, are worshipped at this festival, and the following day is a gala one for herdsmen and *gowalas* (cowherds), among whom Krishna spent his young days.

In some parts of Western India there is a custom whereby one of the worshippers affects to represent the new-born Krishna as a deity named Kanhoba, and, for the time being, he is worshipped by the other devotees. The head of a temple of Kanhoba is termed *Bhagat*, and on this day he works himself into a state of hysteria, and is believed to be possessed by Krishna.

Anant Chaudash. *Anant Chaudash*, or the 14th of Anant, happens on the fourteenth of the light half of Bhadon, and is in honour of *Ananta* or *Sesha*, the king of the serpents, the "Infinite One" on which Vishnu rests during the intervals of creation. In accordance with the rules contained in the *Bhavishya Puran*, a fast is observed and salutation is made to Ganesha and a number of stars, planets, and other gods, both animate and inanimate. The silver and gold cord called Anant is then tied on the arm, and the *puja* terminates after the story of Anant has been read. In the course of this, Krishna says: "I am myself 'Infinity,' and one cannot leave this world until passing out of my endless circle." This circle is represented emblematically by a serpent swallowing itself by the tail, and the armlet is the sign of the *Anant*, to remind the wearer of the immortality of his soul (see also *Naga Panchami*).

Narali Paurnima. *Narali Paurnima* (cocoanut full moon) is observed chiefly by those dwelling by the sea-coast. It is held in Bhadon, when the storms of the monsoon (*mausam*, or season) have abated and the heavy seas have subsided. The cocoanut (*nariyal*) is the especial offering on this occasion; these, in great quantities, along with flowers, are thrown into the sea as oblations to secure its favour.

Ganesha Chaturthi. *Ganesha Chaturthi* occurs in the light half of Bhadrapad in honour of Ganesha, the god with the head of an elephant. Highly gilded images of this deity, riding on his steed, a rat, are first consecrated, and, after being retained for some days in a building, are carried in procession to a river, or pond, or to the sea, and thrown into the water with parting adieus and good wishes. Before consignment to the water the divine spirit is removed from the image by a rite and the recitation of special texts. The Brahmans are feasted during the days of the ceremony.

The Month of Asvin or Asoj.

Pitra Paksha and Amavasya. An *Amavasya* (also called *Ama* and *Darsa Tithi*) is the last day of the dark or waning fortnight of a lunar month, and is considered by the Hindus to be specially set apart for the performance of ceremonies in honour of departed ancestors. It is the "conjunction" of the sun and moon, or the ides of the month.

Of all *Amavasyas* the chief day is *Mahalaya*, the 15th or last day of the moonless fortnight of Kuar or Asvin. The preceding fortnight is called *Pitra Paksha* (ancestors' fortnight). Every day thereof is sacred, and ceremonies are then performed daily in honour of the deceased. Whatever day of the moon a man died, the same day of that fortnight may be observed as his *sraddh*, for which there are special rites.

According to the Shastras, spirits of the departed leave their abode and come to this world during these two weeks in Asvin to receive the worship and homage of their descendants. Spirits of ancestors are usually worshipped before all important domestic ceremonies, for they are believed to be still hovering about their own families. Only those worship them, however, who have lost their fathers, for the spirits cannot pass through mortals to affect their children.

The father, it must be noted, is greatly respected in Hindu families and in former days, if not now, was almost deified.

The **Sraddh** is performed on one day of the fortnight, and the *tarpana*, 'offering of water,' on each day of the fortnight, first to the deceased father and paternal ancestors, then to the mother and her ancestors. The text repeated is—" The Father is heaven, the Father is religion, the Father is the highest form of penance, prayer, and meditation ; it is by pleasing the Father that all the gods are propitiated."

There are strict rules regarding the rites ; they should be performed by the eldest son, or, in his unavoidable absence, by the next son, in a quiet and clean place. Compliance with the rules therefore necessitates marriage and the procreation of sons ; otherwise there would be none to pray for and conciliate the spirits, which would consequently be uneasy and give trouble ; but after two generations they fortunately pass into a state of rest. During *sraddh*, and sometimes for the whole fortnight, no shaving, cutting of the hair, or paring of the nails is permissible.

The Phalgu river in Gaya is a stream particularly sacred to these spirits, and worship performed there helps them into paradise. At certain times a large *Phalgu* fair is held by a pond at Pharral in the neighbourhood of Kurukshetra. Articles are thrown into the river and this pond as offerings to the spirits. The name *Phalgu* seems to mean the 'fructifying quality.'

Durga Puja. This festival is especially celebrated in Bengal, and the *Puja* holidays are enjoyed by immense crowds. The goddess Durga, daughter of the Himalaya mountains and wife of Siva, goes for a ten days' visit to her father's home, and the Shastras say that the festival should be held in the month of Chaitra ; the autumnal festival, however, was inaugurated in the *Ramayana* to celebrate the destruction of the demon-king Ravana with the assistance of Durga, who sent down portions of the Himalayas to make a bridge to Ceylon, dropping bits on the way and thus forming the Vindhya and other mountains.

Durga is the central figure of the *Markandeya Purana.* She is the personification of the creative energy and centre of the universe ; she pursues the demons who wage war against the gods ; ten-armed, she stands on a lion with swords in her hands and subdues her foes, among whom is one with a buffalo-head, named Mahisasura. With her are Kartik, the god of war, Ganesha, the elephant-headed deity who rides on a rat, Sarasvati, the goddess of learning, and Lakshmi, the goddess of love and good fortune. These are the deities of the Durga Puja.

The ceremonies continue for ten days. Throughout the first three days images, sometimes gorgeously decorated, are set up by wealthy people in their houses, where costly entertainments are given. On the seventh day bathing commences and on the final day images are carried in procession with great pomp and immersed in the river. During the ceremonies goats are sacrificed—some substituting pumpkins for the animals—and everyone wears his best clothes. After the immersion, children reverence their elders and are blessed in return; friends embrace and the occasion is one for forgiveness and the settling of differences.

The Shastras prescribe a long series of offerings, fasts, recitations, and sacrifices for the ten days' festival known as *Durga-Ashtami* (tenth day of Durga), and the ceremonies in Northern India chiefly consist of dressing the hair and adorning Durga's image and offering food during the first five days; on the sixth day the goddess is awakened in the *bel* tree in the evening and on the following day she is brought forth and worshipped. Sacrifices commence on the evening of the eighth and continue on the ninth day. Finally, the goddess is dismissed or put to rest on the tenth day, dust and mud are thrown, and thereafter there is great rejoicing.

The form of the festival varies somewhat in different parts of the country.

Dussehra. In the north and west of India the last day is termed *Dussehra* (tenth day), also named *Vijaya Dasmi* (victory tenth day), and is especially observed, for it was then that Rama gained his great victory over Ravana. People polish the instruments of their profession at this time and also clean, plaster, and whitewash their houses and generally put things in order.

The *khaujan*, or wagtail (motacella alba), is looked for and omens taken from its situation, for it bears a holy *tilak* (caste mark); if near lotus flowers or among elephants, cows, horses, or snakes, it forebodes conquest and good luck; if, however, on ashes, bones, or refuse, evil may follow and the gods must be propitiated—Brahmans must be fed and a medicinal bath taken.

In the villages little figures of Durga are made out of cowdung; these are highly decorated and placed on the walls of houses; offerings are made and barley is sown before them; on the eighth or ninth day these are thrown into a river or pond accompanied by shouts of *jae* (victory).

In the towns the tenth day is generally celebrated by the *Ram Lila,* a play performed in an open plain on which is set up a huge wicker-work image of the demon Ravana, filled with fireworks. An enclosure, at some little distance, represents *Lanka* (Ceylon) and the principal events of the rescue of Sita by Rama, as recorded in the *Ramayana,* are acted. Little boys are dressed up as the goddess and monkeys, while Hanuman, the monkey-general, is to be seen, with an enormous tail, acting as a body-guard for the hero. The closing act consists in the advance of Rama in his chariot towards Ravana, against whom he shoots an arrow which causes a series of explosions; the demon catches fire in mysterious fashion, catherine wheels revolve on his head, and he rapidly sinks in a heap of ashes amidst the shouts of the spectators. Sita is then rescued by Rama, and carried off in a chariot with further applause.

The *Dussehra* marks the close of the rains and the four months' absence of the gods; it is the signal, as it were, for the recommencement of joyful festivals of all kinds; further, it has always been specially observed by the military classes, who consider it auspicious to set out on an expedition just afterwards.

Chandra. The last day of the month of Asoj ushers in the Hindu winter, and on this day it is correct to wear only white clothes and silver (*chandi*) ornaments in honour of the Moon (*Chandra*). In the evening, when lamps are lighted, a good Hindu Rajput should seat himself on a white linen cloth and worship his titulary divinity and feed the Brahmans with sugar and milk.

The Month of Kartik.

Bali Pratapada. *Bali Pratapada* is celebrated on the first day of the light half of Kartik in honour of the demon-king Bali, the descendant of Prahlad, who was crushed by Vishnu for trying to displace Indra from his dominion. It seems that certain people of Western India consider him a hero and used to pray that his reign may return. The day is observed by bathing and by the extremely useful practice of clearing away dirt and rubbish from houses; there is also much singing and playing of musical instruments.

Bhratri Dwitya. On the second day following the *amavas*, or ides of Kartik, is the festival of

Bhratri Dwitya (the brothers), so called because the river goddess Yamuna (Jumna) on this day entertained her brother (*bhratri*) Yama. Presents are given by girls to their brothers in celebration of the occasion. When the cattle return from grazing in the evening, the cow is worshipped.

Diwali, *or Dipawali. Dipavali* means 'a row of lights,' and is the great festival of illumination. There are many versions as to its origin. Some say that it commemorates the marriage of Lakshmi, goddess of prosperity, love, and beauty, with the divine Vishnu; in the north-west of India this goddess is certainly connected with the worship which takes place on this day. Others suggest that it celebrates the recovery of the jewelry of Aditi (mother of the gods) by Krishna from a demon named Nakasura, whom he slew, or that it is perhaps in memory of the release of 16,000 maidens whom this demon held as prisoners.

The following interesting account of the festival, as observed in the Eastern Punjab, is given in Ibbetson's Settlement Report, Karnal district, 1883:—

"The ordinary Diwali is on the 14th of Kartik and is called the little Diwali. On this day the *pitr* or ancestors visit the house. But the day after is celebrated the great or Gobardhan Diwali, in which Krishna is worshipped in his capacity of cowherd, and which all owners of cattle should observe. On the day of the little Diwali the whole house is freshly plastered. At night lamps are burnt as usual, and the people sit up all night. Next morning the housewife takes all the sweepings and old clothes in a dust-pan and turns them on to the dunghill, saying '*daladr dur ho*'; *daladr* meaning thriftless, lazy, and therefore poor. Meanwhile the women have made a *Gobardhan* of cowdung, which consists of Krishna lying on his back surrounded by little cottage loaves of dung to represent mountains, bristling with grass stems with tufts of cotton or rag on the top for trees; and little dung balls for cattle, watched by dung men dressed in bits of rag. Another opinion is that the cottage loaves are cattle and the little balls calves. On this is put the churn-staff and five whole sugar canes, and some parched rice and a lighted lamp in the middle. The cowherds are then called in, and they salute the whole and are fed with parched rice and sweets. The Brahman then takes the sugar cane and eats a bit; and till that time nobody must cut, or press, or eat cane.

Parched rice is given to the Brahman; and the bullocks have their horns dyed, and get extra well fed.

Four days before the Diwali or on the 11th Kartik is the Devuthani Gyaras, on which the gods wake up from their four months' sleep, beginning with the 11th Sarh and during which it is forbidden to marry, to cut sugarcane, or to put new string on to bedsteads on pain of a snake biting the sleeper. On the night of this day the children run about the village with lighted sticks and torches."

The annual cleaning which occurs on this occasion in the houses of Hindus is of great utility from a sanitary point of view. At this time the merchants check their accounts, and it is auspicious then to consecrate and open new ledgers.

The illuminations throughout the country supply the most picturesque and enchanting scenes, especially when the lights are reflected over the still water of a tank or the gliding surface of a river such as at Benares; the clear atmosphere of India at this season of the year lends itself to the occasion, and there is no method of illuminating buildings to approach that of minute *chirags* with their twinkling lights, picking out in streaks of fire every line of the houses, temples, and *ghats*.

Where a town is situate on the bank of a river, wicks and oil are placed in small receptacles made of *pan* leaves in coracle shape, and, being lighted, are set afloat and allowed to glide down-stream one after another until they appear like a winding endless string of fairy lamps or stars—a very beautiful symbol of *Ananta*, or 'Eternity.'

Kali Puja. In Bengal the Diwali festival is called *Kali Puja*, and is in honour of that grim goddess; it is there celebrated with fireworks, illumination, feasting, and gambling.

On the 16th of Kartik is a grand festival in Rajputana in honour of the goddess Anna Purna (food full), who is however worshipped in other parts of India more especially in the month of Chait. This goddess is believed to be identical with the "Anna Perenna" of the Romans.

Kartika Paurnima. *Kartika Paurnima* is a festival kept on the full moon of the month of Kartik, in honour of Siva's victory over the demon called Tripurasura.

There is a festival on the 29th of this month in honour of Vishnu's awakening from his four months' slumber, or, figuratively, the emergence of the "Sun" from the clouds of the rainy season.

The Months of Aghan and Poh.

There are no festivals of any importance generally observed in the two months of Aghan and Poh.

Mitra Saptimi. The 7th of Aghan, called *Mitra Saptimi*, is, however, held sacred to the Sun as a form of Vishnu, and on this day the Ganges is said to have descended from the foot of Vishnu and fallen over the head of Iswara (Siva). In imitation thereof his votaries obtain water, if possible, from the Ganges, and pour libations over his emblem, the *linga*.

Champa Shashti. In Western India at Jijuri, near Poona, there is a festival called *Champa Shashti*, which is held on the 6th of the light half of Aghan (or Margasirsha) in praise of a local god called Kanhoba. It is noteworthy merely from the fact that it was here that the great human hook-swinging ceremony used to take place; this barbarous custom was prohibited by the British Government in the middle of the last century.

Champa (michelia champaca) is one of the five flowers with which Kama, the god of love, ornaments his arrow. *Shashti* means sixth.

Koli Diali. In the latter end of December a festival called *Koli Diali* is celebrated in Kulu in honour of a *Devi* named Hirma. The chief ceremony consists in a number of men joining hands in a circle and whirling round until they all go sprawling. In the evening there are illuminations at the hamlets all down the valley of the Beas, and the signal for lighting up is given from a small temple in the old castle at Nagar. Two days later there is a fair at this place in honour of the serpent, from which it derives its name, and on this occasion an enormous straw rope is dragged from the village to the river to commemorate the destruction of the reptile which is said to have once ravaged the country-side.

CHAPTER X.

HINDU FAIRS.

WHEN we consider that almost every great saint or hero has finally devolved into a deity and every remarkable object has gradually acquired a divine connection, it is not surprising that myriads of gods are worshipped by the Hindus, and there is a continuous round of functions to be performed and festivals to be celebrated.

Almost every village in India has its local god and its *bhut* or ghost, while many of them have several; these have to be propitiated by offerings, some on certain week-days and others at various seasons of the year. It is these local deities and ghosts which impress the rustics more than any of the gods of the Hindu trinity, and the worship of these, together with the performance of innumerable ceremonies connected with births, marriages, and deaths, make up the ordinary religious life of the Indian masses, while superstitions regulate much of their daily routine.

A remarkable feature, however, of the religious zeal of Indians is their fondness for making pilgrimages. This practice has arisen since Vedic days and was not prescribed in the law of Manu. It seems to be greatly due to the reverence which came to be paid to the rivers, streams, and ponds, so necessary for the welfare of a people dependent on agriculture. Being of such utility, these waters naturally occupied an important position in the ancient hymns of praise and gradually became deified. All the large rivers, many of the smaller streams, and large numbers of tanks or lakes and ponds are considered of extreme sanctity, and the custom has long existed to visit those places on their banks, which have achieved notoriety from their situation, in order to acquire merit and future reward.

The latter part of Kartik is considered an auspicious time to set out on pilgrimages, for it was then that the great Rama commenced his successful expedition and then that Vishnu returned to the earth after an absence of some four months in the nether regions. From this time forward until the Spring a large proportion of the travelling public in India consists of pilgrims, male and female, on their way to attend one or another of the religious fairs, or to visit sacred places, and bathe in holy waters. At this time thousands proceed to Hardwar, where the sacred Ganges issues from the Himalayas and is supposed to have descended from the head of Siva on to the earth ; there they bathe, perform certain rites, and obtain sealed bottles of the divine liquid, which will later be poured over the idols of Vishnu or Siva, or used at marriage, death, and other ceremonies. Hardwar means literally the 'discharging gate' from *har* (terminalia chebula), a purgative, and *dwara*, a gate. It is situated on the right bank of the Ganges near Roorkee. Every twelfth year the *Kumbh Mela*, as it is called, assumes large proportions.

At Nathdwara, the 'Door of God,' is situate a most celebrated temple of Krishna, the Apollo of the Hindus. This place is about twenty-two miles from Oodipur on the right bank of the Bunas. It owes its distinction to the fact that it contains an image of this god which is said to be the same that has been worshipped at Mathura ever since his deification some eleven hundred years before Christ.

Among the most sacred places of pilgrimage must be mentioned *Benares*, that city of temples and stronghold of Siva worship; others specially connected with the Ganges are *Badari Kedar* near its source, *Ganga Sagar* at the point where it flows into the ocean (as its name implies), and *Prayag* (Allahabad) at its confluence with the Jumna, where as many as half a million pilgrims assemble annually during the *Magh Mela* to bathe in the essence of sanctity formed by the combined streams.

The *Cave of Amar Nath* amidst the snows of the Himalayas in Kashmir, the shrine of *Mahadeo* in a gorge of the Mahadeo Hills near Pachmarhi, and *Omkar* on an island in the Nerbudda are notable in connection with the worship of Siva, while *Jowala Mukhi* in the Punjab is remarkable as the spot where Sati, wife of Siva, is said to have burnt herself.

Citrakut in Bundelkund, *Ramesvar* on an island between India and Ceylon, and *Nasik* on the

Godavari are among the places famous in connection with the adventures of the hero Rama.

Kurukshetra, on the Sarasvati to the north of Delhi, is the centre of the field of Kuru, referred to in the *Mahabharata*, and also the birthplace of Hinduism.

Besides the ordinary pilgrims who attend the great fairs and visit holy places, there are thousands of ascetics or *sadhus*; these extraordinary mortals form separate little groups of their own sects at the fairs, and squat on mats or platforms under quaint umbrellas or beneath trees and bushes; there they perform the actions prescribed by their respective creeds; some reading or reciting, others meditating, and yet others undergoing dreadful austerities.

At most sacred places the local Brahmans maintain huge registers in which they record particulars of the persons for whom they officiate; they arrange for the accommodation of their clients during their visit, perform the necessary rites for them, and attend to repeat texts while they are bathing, and to collect offerings from one and all. It is considered of great importance that a man should be attended by the same Brahman, or his successor, who officiated for his ancestors, and the registers are arranged with indices to facilitate search. The Brahmans reap a rich harvest in fees and offerings on these occasions.

By bathing in holy water a Hindu receives absolution and merit; in some instances he thereby ensures rapid caste promotion in future lives. If he should happily die while bathing in the holy of holies at Benares, or such like spot, his soul in all probability unites immediately with the Supreme Being.

Most of the large bathing fairs resemble one another, so a description of one does for many.

Just south of the town of Thanesar is a large lake called *Tirath Kurukshetra*, or 'Field of Kuru,' an ancestor of the heroes of the Mahabharata, who is said to have become an ascetic on its banks. Within a few hundred yards is another smaller lake known as *Saniahet* (*Sannihit*, or 'secret concentration'); around these, for a distance varying from 15 to 30 miles, there is a holy tract within the confines of which are about 360 sacred places visited by pilgrims.

At the time of an eclipse of the sun it is believed that the waters of all other sacred ponds within that area concentrate in Saniahet. Now the common idea is that on this occasion the sun is obscured by a black, filthy, and mischievous demon who takes possession of the moon and blots out the light of the sun; to escape from the evil effect of the subdued light it is necessary to bathe in holy water, and one of the most efficacious places to do so is Saniahet. Gatherings, which sometimes amount to half a million people, assemble around the two lakes, and, during the short time of the transit, their object is to immerse themselves in both of them.

The religious enthusiasm during the bathing is immense, and it is a marvellous sight—the vast crowds moving with haste between the two lakes—that mass of humanity splashing at the hundreds of *ghats*—that march of thousands of pilgrims, solemn at first, more and more excited as they approach the steps leading to the sacred water, and at the supreme moment their faces beaming with intense religious joy and gladness. The only sounds to be heard are the dripping of the water, the subdued hum of muttered prayer, the occasional tinkle of bells or noise of melodious horns; the only active movements to be seen are those of the arms of bathers as they souse themselves with water and of the Brahmans as they flit here and there amidst the multitude, holding out little brass vessels to receive the offerings of ornaments and coin.

Let us now leave this scene and glance at another, high up in the Himalayas in the east of Kashmir.

The *Cave of Amar Nath* is situate in a long glacial gorge, and thousands of pilgrims visit it during the month of Sawan. It contains a huge perpetual icicle, which is said to wax and wane with the moon and is regarded as a *linga* and most miraculous emblem of Siva the Destroyer.

The pilgrimage consists of eight stages, ninety-one miles in all, stretching from Srinagar, by Pahelgam and Panchaterani, to Amar Nath. On the 11th of the bright half of Sawan all the pilgrims collect at Pahelgam and on the following day march up into the snow. Some are poorly clad, others practically nude, and the determination required by these enthusiasts to perform this arduous journey can hardly be imagined. Formerly large numbers died by the way through cold and privation, but nowadays the Kashmir State assists the pilgrims by providing food for the poorer classes and *sadhus*, and resting places or refuge huts for the weary or sick; the route leading to Amar Nath has been greatly, improved and is no longer the rough track which it was in former days.

In Central India there is another gorge which contains a notable shrine of *Mahadeo*, one of the names of Siva; it is situate near Pachmarhi in the Mahadeo Hills. Once a year pilgrims encamp at the foot of the hills and then wend their way upwards by several rugged tracks to the shrine which rests in a cave, running about a hundred yards into the bowels of the earth and entered through a huge arch in the sandstone cliff. A stream of clear water gushes forth from a cleft in the rock at the end of the cave, and at this point stands a small conical stone, or *linga*, the symbol of the great god.

A huge bell tolls while strings of pilgrims pass to and fro, making offerings of all the money and ornaments in their possession and presenting little bottles to the Brahmans to be filled with sacred water and sealed for them to carry home. Formerly the journey was dangerous on account of the presence of tigers and other wild animals, but these are now few and far between.

At *Omkar-Mandhatta* the local Sivite gospel relates that devotees, who cast themselves from a certain high precipice on to the rocks below to fulfil special oaths, would marry daughters of the angels and receive absolution for all sins, even for the slaying of a Brahman—the worst possible offence. This barbarous practice, together with hook-swinging, *suttee*, and the offering of human beings as sacrifices and of women as slaves or concubines, has long since been prohibited.

At a place named *Katas* in the Salt Range of the Punjab lies a holy tank where a large *mela* (assemblage) is held every year in honour of the goddess *Sati* (Suttee). The story runs that, when she died, Siva was so grieved that the tears rained from his eyes and from one of them a pool was formed at Pokhar, near Ajmer, and from the other the spring at Katas (an abruption of *Kataksha* or 'Raining Eye') came into existence.

One of the most venerated shrines in India is the *Temple of Jagannath* at Puri in Orissa, where Vishnu is especially worshipped and the great *Car Festival* is celebrated every year. Regarding this an article in the *Times of India Illustrated Weekly* relates:—"No fewer than sixty-two festivals are held in Puri during the year, the most important of which is the *Rath Jattra*, or 'Car Festival,' held about the end of June. Immediately preceding this is the *Snan-Jattra*, when the god is said to have fever and is not visible for fifteen days, though, as a matter of fact, the images are being cleaned up for their public appearance during the forthcoming festival.

During the Rath Jattra the three images are brought out of the temple by the Lion Gate and placed on huge cars specially built for the occasion. These cars are enormous chariots of wood and bamboo, gaily bedecked with gaudy cloths and spangles, each running on sixteen solid wooden wheels. The car of Jagannath is forty-five feet in height with wheels seven feet in diameter, while the other cars are only slightly less in dimensions.

When the images have been placed in the cars they are given golden hands and feet and dressed in rich raiment, and the procession is then ready to start off on its journey down the Bara Dand or Big Road to Jagannath's Garden House. When first they see the images the pilgrims bow themselves down to the ground, then seize the cars, and drag them along. The Great Road is packed with crowds of enthusiastic pilgrims, and the cars may take anything from six hours to three days to traverse its length of a mile and a half.

It was during this slow procession that fanatical pilgrims, being carried away by their religious fervour, were said to have thrown themselves before the chariots of the gods and by sacrificing their lives to have won a direct way to heaven. It is more than doubtful, however, whether the majority of these sacrifices were not more accidental than real. For with a crowd of some hundred thousand pilgrims, many of whom are women, all pressing forward to catch a sight of their deity, and struggling to obtain a share in the honour of drawing the car, it is not to be wondered at if a certain number are pushed beneath the massive wheels and killed. But fortunately, in recent years, the authorities have taken such good precautions that these accidents now rarely happen.

Arrived at the garden the images are carried into the temple, where they remain for seven days, at the end of which time they again return to the Great Temple in their chariots. But by this time most of the pilgrims have returned to their houses, and far from being a triumphal procession it is often a matter of some difficulty to obtain sufficient labour to drag the huge cars home again."

The popular legend regarding the origin of Jagannath is somewhat complicated. For a long time in the golden age men had been vainly searching for the god Vishnu until finally a king named Indradyumna sent out Brahmans to the four quarters to try and find him; three returned unsuccessful, but the fourth, who had gone towards the east, arrived at the dwelling of a fowler named Basu, who compelled him to marry his daughter and remain there to bring honour to his family. Now Basu was a servant to Jagannath, the Lord of the World, and he daily offered fruit and flowers to his god secretly in the wilderness. One day the Brahman managed to obtain a view of Jagannath, who was in the form of a blue stone image (of which there are many in Orissa formed of common chlorite).

A vision appeared in the shape of a crow and directed the Brahman to carry the news to the king. When Indradyumna at length heard of this, he set out with a vast army, forced his way through the dense jungle, and, reaching the Blue Mountain near the spot, became so overwhelmed with pride that he cried: "Who is like unto me, whom the Lord of the World has chosen to build his temple, and to teach men to call on his name?" The lord Jagannath was exceeding wroth at the king's conceit, and declared that he should certainly construct the temple but would have to seek anew for his god. The temple was accordingly erected, but Indradyumna passed away to heaven without discovering the whereabouts of Jagannath.

Many ages later, when the sacred edifice had been buried in the sands, and the city, which had sprung up around it, had crumbled into ruins, the king of the place was riding along the beach when his horse stumbled upon the pinnacle of the forgotten shrine; on having the sand cleared away he found the temple of Jagannath fair and fresh as when first built.

Indradyumna, who had been undergoing penance in heaven, at length prevailed upon Brahmā to reveal the spot where Jagannath was concealed, and the Lord of the World, appearing in a vision, showed him his image as a huge block of timber thrown up by the sea upon the beach.

All the carpenters of the kingdom were summoned to fashion the block into the likeness of

Jagannath, and finally, with the assistance of Vishnu, this was achieved. The king of the land then secured the aid of Basu, the old fowler, to convey the god to the temple which Indradyumna had prepared for him, and there it was locked up for a rest, the king declaring that no one should enter for twenty-one days. The queen, however, persuaded him to let her have a peep in order that she might be preserved from barrenness, and, on her doing so, it was found that there were images of Jagannath, his brother, and sister; but they were only fashioned from the waist upwards, while the two gods only had stumps for arms and the sister had none at all. So they remain to this day, but on the occasion of festivals golden arms are provided.

Kulu, the sub-division of the Kangra district in the Punjab, is perhaps favoured with more fairs than any other tract in India. There nearly every hamlet has at least one during the hot season, in addition to the ordinary festivals, and the dates are conveniently arranged so that they do not clash. Once a year during the month of Asoj there is a great parade of all the godlings of the neighbourhood in honour of the god Ragganath at Sultanpur, the old capital of Kulu. On this occasion there is a *rath* festival somewhat similar to that which takes place at Puri. The god is conveyed from his temple in a highly decorated vehicle, drawn by the people themselves and escorted by all the minor deities, to a spot where a tent is erected for his stay of five days; this period is occupied by the godlings in paying visits to one another in the presence of gaily dressed men and women, who dance, sing, beat drums, and play unmusical instruments far into the night throughout the ceremonies. On the last day of the fair, Ragganath again ascends his chariot and, escorted as before, proceeds to the bank of the Beas ; here a buffalo and other animals are sacrificed and a figure representing Lanka (or is it Ravana ?) is beheaded to celebrate the triumph of Ragganath, in his shape as Rama, over the demons of Ceylon. The car is thereafter drawn to the bank of the Sarwari stream, across which the idol is conveyed in a palanquin and finally put to rest in his temple. The minor gods thereupon betake themselves to their respective homes.

Ragganath makes another public appearance in Baisakh when he is conveyed to the Beas for a bathe.

Many of the great religious fairs are to the people of India very much what cattle-shows and gipsy fairs are to the rustics in England—an occasion which is made an excuse for an outing or a "week end." There are the same kinds of peep-shows, merry-go-rounds, circuses, theatres, and even cinemas, all on a small scale in tiny booths. Music is provided by gramaphones, *Angrezi bajas* (English bands), and quaint Indian instruments, some of which bear a distant resemblance to the bagpipe.

Rows of little temporary shops contain trinkets, knick-knacks, and toys to delight the women and children ; others are filled with fancy articles of every description ; the grain-merchants do a roaring trade, likewise the stall-keepers who sell food and drink.

At other gatherings, however, such as those in the Mahadeo gorge or at the cave of Amar Nath, there is none of this merry-making ; men and women are there merely intent on performing a meritorious act, whereby they will receive compensation in a future existence.

CHAPTER XI.

HINDU SECTS AND SOCIETIES.

INDIA is, par excellence, the land of asceticism and *sadhus*, or persons who belong to the numerous ascetic sects and orders of Hinduism.

The sects may be roughly divided into three main groups :—

1. *Vaishnavas*, or those who worship Vishnu, or his manifestations in some form or other.
2. *Saivas*, who in various ways show devotion to Siva.
3. *Miscellaneous*.

It is noticeable that there are practically no *sadhus* who worship Brahmā, the first member of the Hindu trinity.

The members of the various orders or fraternities may be identified almost invariably by the *tilak*, or mark, which, like Cain, they bear upon their foreheads ; sometimes they are distinguished still further by signs and emblems which are painted, or even branded, on their persons ; most of them carry rosaries and wear necklaces. The rosaries are either made of agates, cornelians, and other stones, or of *rudraksha* (Rudra's eye) berries, those of the Saivas having 32 or 64 berries and those of the Vaishnavas as many as 108. These numbers are said to be multiplications of the number of signs of the zodiac by that of certain celestial bodies. A Vaishnava, however, whom I once questioned, informed me that his beads represented the 108 heads of Ravana which were struck off by Rama.

The *tilak* of the Vaishnava sects is usually composed of three upright marks called the *trifala*, which is emblematic of the three gods of the trinity ; the two outer ones are white or yellow and sometimes slant outwards, while the central one is red. The white lines are painted with a peculiar clay, which is called *gopi chandana* after the milk-maids of Dwarka, whence it is obtained ; the red pigment is a mixture of turmeric and lime.

The Saivas favour the *tripundra*, which consists of three horizontal lines painted with ashes.

Many of the *sadhus* smear themselves with ashes or clay, and, when not practically naked, wear orange or salmon-coloured garments, or adorn themselves in "sackcloth and ashes." Few carry out any of the ordinary "caste" observances, for they mostly regard themselves as separate from worldly concerns.

Vast numbers of these people continually perambulate the country, visiting the various holy fairs and sacred places ; some are attached to monasteries under *mahants* and proceed on long journeys, receiving alms and collecting news, for delivery, on their return, to their respective head priests ; others set up as hermits, or undergo most terrible austerities ; and there are those who affect the guise of *sadhus* for evil purposes, or gain, or out of laziness.

It is sad to think what an enormous tax these people place upon the country. The census of 1911 shows that, out of a total population of 313,000,000 in the whole of India, over 3,000,000 are beggars or vagrants. If we take ten rupees per annum as a very low estimate of the cost of maintenance of each of these creatures, we find that India is spending £2,000,000 on them every year. We must remember too that the priestly classes, which account for over 2,700,000 of the people, take from the laymen an enormous dole, for which certainly the 700,000 give nothing in return in the shape of religious ministration; £3,000,000 more may be reckoned safely as the contribution for their support at about Rs. 60 per annum for each. In this manner probably over £5,000,000 are spent on worthless members of society—persons who are bound up in themselves, who exist on the toil of others, who eat food produced by others, who even wear symbols and carry articles made by others—and these dependents, these ascetics forsooth, profess to have removed themselves from worldly cares and to be in union, or approaching union, with the Divine Being.

The three main divisions of ascetics contain numerous sects, of which brief notes are given below.

Vaishnavas.

1. *Ramanujas*, or *Sri Vaishnavas*, are followers of Ramanuja, and worship Sri or Lakshmi, wife of

Vishnu. They are mostly found in the Deccan. The members are particular about their food, which each has to prepare privately for himself. They paint on their bodies, in white clay and red patches, emblems of Vishnu, such as the lotus, conch, and discus. They retain the sacred thread, carry rosaries, and wear orange-coloured clothes. Their *tilak* is the *trifala* with a connecting streak across the top of the nose. They follow doctrines from Vedanta works and the Puranas.

2. *Ramanandis, Ramavats,* or *Ramats.* This sect is chiefly encountered in the Gangetic plains, where they possess well-endowed monasteries. They worship Rama and Sita chiefly, but also Rama's brothers and Hanuman. The members of their principal sub-sects are called Bairagis, and Sanyasis; two others are known as Achari and Khaki.

The *Bairagis* (a name common to most Vaishnava *sadhus*) do not wear coloured clothes; they have emblems of Vishnu branded on their right arms, and are fond of head-cloths on which the names Rama and Sita are printed.

The *Sanyasis,* who must not be confused with those of the Saiva group, robe themselves in salmon-coloured clothes of cotton; the *Acharis* wear garments made of silk and wool; and the *Khakis,* who are generally naked, smear themselves with ashes.

All Ramanandis have the *trifala* as their sect mark, carry rosaries, and wear the sacred thread, whether they were previously entitled to do so or not.

3. *Kabir-panthis*, who are followers of Kabir, the chief of Ramananda's twelve disciples, are found mostly in Upper and Central India. They believe in a Supreme Being, who can assume shapes, such as Vishnu, and has occasionally become incarnate in mortals, such as Rama. They use a form of the *trifala* for a *tilak*. Any caste may join the sect, which is inoffensive.

4. *Ballabh-acharyas*, or *Rudra-sampradayins*, follow doctrines from the Bhagavata Purana and Ballabha's works. They worship the cowherd Bala Gopala. All castes, except the very lowest, can join the sect, and the members do not practise austerities but indulge in good feeding and drinking, while some actually surrender their women-folk to their gurus, or *Maharajas* as they are called, whom they regard as demi-gods.

5. *Madhvas*, or *Brahma-sampradayins*, are found in the south of India. This sect was founded by Madhav-acharya. The members wear an orange-coloured cloth round their loins, brand their persons with emblems of Vishnu, but discard the sacred thread. All castes are admitted, but only a Brahman can become a guru. They generally reside in monasteries, and differ from true Vaishnavas in that they worship Siva, Durga, and Ganesha, as well as Vishnu, and deny the absorption of the worldly soul into the Supreme Spirit.

6. *Chaitanya's* followers are mostly in Bengal. He was regarded as an incarnation of Krishna, to whom they show great devotion. All castes, even

the lowest, and both sexes can enter this sect. They are usually called *Bairagis*. The males and females frequently live as man and wife, while those of the sub-sects *Sahaja, Spashta Dayaka*, and *Baul* live together promiscuously and lead most immoral lives.

7. *Dadu-panthis* are followers of a low-caste man named Dadu and worship Rama. The *Naga-panthis* are a sub-sect; they have no *tilak*, but wear a sort of small cap.

Saivas.

1. *Dandis* are so called, because each member carries a staff as an emblem of Siva. They either go naked or wear salmon-coloured garments. Only Brahmans can join the sect, and they must receive their food only from the same. They are said to consider themselves part and parcel of the god Siva.

2. *Sanyasis*, or *Dasnamis*, are all vegetarians. Any Hindu may be a member. They bear no distinctive sect mark, unless it be the eye of Siva in the centre of the forehead. These *sadhus* generally have long matted hair, and always carry a pair of iron tongs and wear a necklace of *rudraksha* berries, which are peculiarly sacred to Siva. They smear their bodies with ashes, wear tiger or leopard skins, and never put on white clothes. Many well-known reformers and leaders of thought were for a time members of this sect.

3. *Yogis*, or *Jogis*, practise suppression of the breath, deep meditation, fixing of the eyes, and a great variety of postures, in order, as they believe,

to effect *Yoga* or 'union' with the Divine Spirit. They are meat-eaters and wine-drinkers and wear rosaries of *rudraksha* berries. Many of them profess superhuman powers. Any caste may join the sect. The members either go nude or wear saffron-coloured clothes, and they coil their matted hair on the top of their heads.

4. The *Kanphatis* (bored ears) are a branch of this sect, who bore large holes in their ears and wear huge earrings of glass, jade, or wood.

Yogaism has obtained some notice outside India, but it lends itself to imposture, and many who set themselves up as Yogis are rogues of the deepest dye.

5. *Paràma-hansas,* literally 'supreme geese,' claim union of the world-soul with the Divine Spirit. Both Saivas and Vaishnavas undergo a lengthy probationership in order to qualify for membership of this order, which is considered the highest in asceticism. They perform severe austerities.

6. *Aghoris* and their female consorts *Aghorinis* are ghouls in human shape, but, fortunately, few in number. They propitiate Siva by revolting practices, such as eating offal, carrion, and the flesh of corpses. Their belief is that, as the Divine Being is manifest in everything, nothing can be impure, and they live up to their creed by devouring things which are ordinarily regarded as foul and disgusting.

7. *Urdha-bahus* extend one or both arms above their heads until the flesh withers away and the joints become fixed.

8. *Urdha-mukhis* suspend themselves by the feet and hang head downwards. They will remain in this position, sometimes for half an hour at a time, while swinging over a fire. After this austerity they are massaged by their companions for about an hour, when they are ready for another suspension.

9. *Akasa-mukhins* keep their necks bent back and gaze at the sky.

Miscellaneous.

1. *Saktas* worship the *Sakti* or 'female energy,' and have, as their special deities, the wives of Siva. Their symbol is the *yoni*, or female emblem. The sect consists of two main branches, the "right hand" and the "left hand" worshippers. The chief difference between the two is that the former do not indulge in such obscene practices as the latter, whose tenets actually require the observance of rites in which women, flesh, wine, fish, and magical signs take a part. The goddess is represented at the ceremonies by nude women, and, with these requirements, it is natural that the so-called worship has degenerated into loathsome impurity.

This sect is not common, but is to be found here and there in India, especially in Bengal, but the members have to indulge in their rites with secrecy. The extreme members are called *Kowls*, and paint their foreheads with vermilion.

2. *Sauryas*, or *Sauras*, are worshippers of *Surya*, or the 'sun'. They, however, adore Rama and other gods.

3. *Gosains* (from Sanskrit *go-swami* or 'Lord of the Cow'). This term is applied to certain religious mendicants, monks, and guardians of temples, also as a caste name for a class of laymen.

4. *Ganapatyas* form a sect for the worship of Ganesha, or Ganapati.

Hindu Societies.

The *Samaj*, or Hindu Society, is a creation of the 19th century, during which there was naturally an influx of Western ideas. Numerous leaders of thought arose and attempted to purify and arrange the Hindu beliefs, so as to bring them into line with modern requirements.

The first of these reformers of any importance was Ram Mohan Roy, who had considerable intercourse with Europeans and devoted much time to the study of Christianity. Before his death, which occurred in England in 1833, he founded the *Brahma Samaj*. The tenets of this society, as framed some ten years later under the direction of Debendernath Tagore, were the abandonment of idolatry, the worship of one God, and the retention of ancient customs in so far as they did not clash with the foregoing.

Between 1857 and 1866 a member of this society, named Keshab Chandar Sen, disagreed with Debendernath over certain matters and became the leader of a new branch which rejects the

Veda; the creed as finally formulated by him was:—

1. One God, one scripture, one church.
2. Eternal progress of the soul.
3. Communion of prophets and saints.
4. Fatherhood and Motherhood of God.
5. Brotherhood of man and Sisterhood of woman.
6. Harmony of knowledge and holiness, love and work, *Yoga* and asceticism in their highest development.
7. Loyalty to Sovereign.

The *Prarthana Samaj*, or 'Prayer Society,' was started in Bombay as a result of the new doctrines, and has the following tenets:—

1. Belief in one God.
2. Renunciation of idolatry
3. Moral living.
4. Repentance of sins.
5. Prayer to God for pardon.

About the same time another somewhat similar society, called the *Veda Samaj*, was formed in Madras, and later on this became the *Brahma Samaj* of Southern India.

Another offshoot was the *Sadharana Brahma Samaj*.

Owing to all these dissensions the movement started by Ram Mohan Roy has made little progress, but such as it has achieved has been sound, especially in elevating the position of women.

The *Arya Samaj* is another reforming society. It was founded by Dayananda Sarasvati, who was originally a Brahman of Kathiawar, but received this name on becoming a Sanyasi. He gave up asceticism and attempted to rebuild the beliefs of the ancient Aryans on the lines of the Veda, to abolish idolatry, to unite the Hindus in a common belief, and to eradicate other religions. By 1880 he had obtained a number of followers, and they now amount to about 250,000, chiefly in the Punjab and United Provinces. The tenets of the society inculcate the following beliefs :—

1. God is the creator, the infinite and almighty, the just and merciful, the omnipresent and incorporeal.

2. God is the source of true knowledge, and he alone may be worshipped and prayed to.

3. The Veda contains true knowledge.

The rules for Aryas, as the members are called, include :—

1. Practise righteousness and justice; love and help one another.

2. Advance knowledge and abolish ignorance.

3. Improve the spiritual, physical, and social status of human beings.

4. Work for the welfare of the society.

There are thus three main ideas, namely :—

(*a*) Belief in one God.

(*b*) Abolition of idolatry.

(*c*) Missionary efforts to spread the beliefs.

The Aryas are doing much for the education and advance of their womanhood, and most of their doctrines are sound, but they include a practice called *niyoga*, or the temporary union of a man and woman for the procreation of children when marriage has failed to produce them, or during the enforced absence of the husband.

The scripture of the Arya Samajists consists of writings by Dayanand brought together in a book known as the *Satyārath Prakāsh.* The society possesses institutions, or *gurukuls*, in which youths are secluded from the age of 8 to 25 and taught the principles of the Arya religion.

Hindu Religious Revival.—The following speech was delivered by the Maharajà Bahadur of Darbhanga, when presiding at the *Sanatana Dharma* public meeting held at Bombay on the 20th December, 1915; it is interesting as showing the efforts being made for a Hindu religious revival :—

"Throwing back our thoughts to the past and looking at the various civilizations that history unfolds before our wondering eyes, and realising that the Hindu civilization is one of the most ancient civilizations that have become known to mankind, we, as Hindus, note with the most joyous and grateful satisfaction that, while mighty States and civilizations like the Egyptian, and Assyrian, the Babylonian, the Greek, the Roman, and many another have come and have gone, our hoary Hindu civilization still lives, thrives, and flourishes, and offers to the world a standing example of the lasting and stately edifice that can be reared on the solid foundations of a truly spiritual religion. The foundations of our civilization have been firmly and truly laid on our ancient Vaidika religion, that *Sanatana Dharma,* the oldest of living religions, which stands unrivalled for the depths of its spirituality as it shines unequalled with the splendour of its philosophy, and yields to none in the purity of its ethics as well as in the flexibility and varied adaptation of its ritual and ceremonies. It has been well and truly said that the *Vaidika Dharma* is like a river, which has shallows that a child may play in, and depths which the strongest diver cannot fathom."

After outlining the nature of the Varnas and Ashramas, His Highness continued :—" Bewitched by the glare of modern Western civilization we are likely to think the caste system as an obstacle to our progress, but those who hold such views seem to forget that the West is as yet trying and experimenting, and has not succeeded in solving its pressing social problems. Western civilization, dominated as it is by the spirit of competition, accentuates the separative tendencies of man. By training the individual to battle for his individual rights, it fosters those disruptive forces which make social stability almost impossible. The hostility between the privileged classes and the aggrieved masses of the feudal times, which brought about the French Revolution, is finding its counterpart to-day in the strife between Capital and Labour. Nor can the schemes of the socialists much help to evolve social peace and harmony out of this ceaseless strife. If we ponder over all this, we cannot but feel grateful to the holy Rishis of yore who devised this system of castes and Ashramas. It trained its votaries to look to their duties and to discharge them fearlessly.

"They had every reason to be proud of their great spiritual inheritance. The time, gentlemen, has come when the Hindus of different classes and denominations must be provided with a common meeting ground where they should be able to feel that they are Hindus first and foremost, and Vaishnavas, Saivas, or Saktas only afterwards; where they should be able to sink and forget minor differences and meet together, in amity and unity, on the firm ground of the basic verities of Hindu religion and philosophy. It was essential that they should not, as Professor Huxley remarked, 'forget the forest in the trees.'"

His Highness dwelt on "these basic, spiritual and ethical unities which are and should ever remain the common belief of all Hindus," and, continuing, said:—"Our revered Rishis, realising the unity of all knowledge, knew no distinction between science, philosophy, and religion. They understood all these to be parts of one great whole, and a study of modern science and philosophy, undertaken with the object of a better understanding of our own scriptures and of leading the mind up to the higher knowledge, the *Para-Vidya*, the knowledge of the Supreme Existence, would not only be profitable, but would be of the utmost use in these days when the streams of Western culture are intermingling closely with ancient Eastern thought. Institutions and gatherings, such as I have the honour of requesting you to start and maintain, will be of admirable help in ensuring a harmonious coalition of the practical West with the philosophical East, and in helping us, without harm or injury to our own glorious spirituality, religion, and philosophy, to assimilate whatever is useful and profitable in the culture and learning which our benign rulers have placed at our disposal. In this way we shall be guarding against any risk of the strong and attractive currents of Western civilization effacing aught that is beautiful and grand in our own ancient Hindu culture. In this connection I may draw your attention once more to the supreme necessity of combining religious instruction with secular education, so as to ensure an all-round growth and avert the dangers of a lop-sided education, training the intellect without a corresponding culture of the emotion and unfoldment of the spiritual nature of man. You must have all been pleased and grateful to our kind rulers for having allowed us to establish the Hindu University where Western training and Hindu religious education shall go hand in hand and co-operate for the turning out of noble Hindu youths, combining in themselves the best points of modern Western culture and of ancient Hindu spirituality.

"Loyalty to the King is natural to the Hindus as it is enjoined by their scriptures. Both by protecting the subjects from outside invasions and by keeping order in the country as well as by protecting the weak from the strong he makes it possible for millions of human beings to lead peaceful lives. Under the benign British rule we have been long enjoying continuous peace, and this very meeting to concert measures for the noble ideals and traditions of the *Sanatana Dharma* is made possible because there is peace in the country, and it is but natural that we should feel grateful to the Gracious King-Emperor who has given us these blessings. It was indeed a divinely inspired act of British statesmanship that prompted our rulers to recognise the genius of our religion and culture and to make religious tolerance and neutrality a basic principle of their rule. By proclaiming non-interference in matters of faith and strictly adhering to that principle, they laid the foundation of their rule broad and deep. For us, Hindus, those who are not against us are with us, and, though Government have been strictly adhering to this principle of religious neutrality, we have ample evidence that it has been benevolent neutrality ; the most striking and convincing proof whereof has been the keen interest shown by the Government in the cultivation of Sanskrit literature and the recent act of His Excellency the Viceroy and the Government of India in giving us the Hindu University. Is it not, therefore, in accordance with the basic ideas of our religion that we should ever be grateful to our benign rulers, and will not our joint loyalty find deeper expression if we have a common prayer for the King-Emperor, as was resolved upon by the All-India Sanatana Dharma Sammilan (Conference) held at Hardwar during the last Kumbha Mela? This will give a fresh life to Hinduism, an impetus which will bear it through in the changed circumstances of the time, when the East cannot ignore the West and the West cannot ignore the East. One of the objects of this gathering is to discuss the form which that common prayer should take, and the different proposals and suggestions would be finally considered at the next sitting of the All-India Hindu Conference to be held at Mattura from the 22nd to the 26th March, 1916, which will ultimately decide as to the form to be accepted by all."

The *Dev Samaj* is a society founded in 1887 at Lahore by Sri Dev Guru Bhagwan, a Brahman of the Cawnpore district. The members believe that the universe consists of matter and force, which are indestructible and have existed eternally. Force by its own motion produces change in matter and becomes changed itself; in this manner living and non-living forms appear and disappear. There is no Creator and no Supreme Being. Matter is divided into four parts namely:—Inorganic substances, vegetables, animals, and mankind; all of these are closely connected, and the last three gradually evolve out of the first. Man's life-force is his soul, and this, with his body, being part of the universe, is subject to the law of change. The soul can thus develop for better or for worse according to the forces which affect it. If the soul has strength, it assumes a finer form after the death of the body, and, if it is weak, it is liable to become extinct, but it can go through transformation.

The object of a member must be to obtain such high development of his soul that it will enter the highest life and thus obtain freedom from the power of all degenerating forces. Persons, who fulfil certain conditions, are admitted to the society on taking a number of vows regarding the leading of a moral life and the observation of certain social rules, which include the proper upbringing and education of male and female children, the helping of others irrespective of caste, creed, or colour.

The Modern Hindu. A large proportion of those Hindus who have received education on Western lines have abandoned their belief in the gods of Hinduism; numbers have given up many of the old customs, such as the wearing of the *choti*, and do not take part in the periodical fairs and festivals; some merely believe in the existence of a Supreme Being and perhaps in transmigration of souls; others attempt to accommodate their systems to the needs of modern times.

CHAPTER XII.

BUDDHISM.

The Foundation of Buddhism.

WHEN Brahmanism had obtained a firm footing in India, there arose a new religion in the shape of Buddhism, which announced that man has the power of acquiring his own salvation and consequently has no use for the Veda.

This belief is said to have been founded by Gautama, who was afterwards known as *Buddha*, or 'The Enlightened,' and sometimes as *Sakya-muni*, which means the 'Sakya Sage.'

Gautama was the son of a king named Suddhodana, who reigned over the Sakya people in Kapilavastu, the capital of a country in the north of India, just south of the present kingdom of Nepal.

Buddhism was not to the liking of Brahmans, for it tended to challenge their authority ; moreover, Gautama's family belonged to the Kshatriya class, and, according to "caste" rules, he had no right to set up as a religious instructor. It spread rapidly, however, during his lifetime in the neighbourhood of his birth-place, and afterwards, for more than a thousand years, continued as a formidable rival to Brahmanism throughout India, but it was then almost entirely ousted from this country, after having established itself in the greater portion of the rest of Asia, where it yet remains the religion, or part of the religion, of over five hundred millions of people. It is still professed by the Burmese, and it lingers in the south-east of Bengal and in the Himalayas near Tibet and Nepal. For these reasons, and because its birth-place was in India proper, Buddhism is dealt with among the "Faiths of India."

There is some uncertainty about the exact date of Gautama's birth, but he is generally believed to have been born about 557 B.C. From an early age he indulged in meditation, instead of joining in games with other boys and amusing himself after the fashion of young princes; as a youth he displayed some skill in manly sports and at the age of nineteen, in the manner then usual, won his wife at a tournament of chiefs. Ten years later his only son, Rahula, was born, and it was at this time that he decided to forsake his home and become an ascetic in the jungle. One evening, having discarded his princely robes and shaved his head, he clothed himself in rags, mounted a horse, and set off with a single attendant. After riding throughout the night he sent the man home with his steed and proceeded on foot alone, to lead thenceforth the life of a religious mendicant. This act was regarded as extremely meritorious and virtuous, and the event is known as the "Great Renunciation."

For a year or so, Gautama attached himself to two Brahman teachers, and then, for the space of six years, he practised austerities in a forest near Gaya, along with five other ascetics. This period of self-mortification, however, brought him no satisfaction; he had not discovered the secret of the soul; he could retain no peace of mind while the problem remained unsolved, and towards the end, he developed a state of religious despair, during which he was forsaken by his five companions. Great was the relief which finally came to him when, sitting beneath a Bo-tree (*Pipul,* ficus religiosa), or the "tree of knowledge," he suddenly became "enlightened" regarding the "Great Truth," which was to influence so many millions of his fellow-creatures.

The idea which had thus entered the mind of Buddha—as he may now be called—consisted of four parts: Worldly existence must always be painful; suffering is caused by desire; this can only be terminated by attaining the state of *Nirvana,* or "extinction of the soul"; such can be achieved by good conduct.

The belief, which thus arose, recognizes no Supreme God, and god is only what man himself can become by his own acts, or *karma.* Transmigration of the soul through a series of bodies was, however, admitted.

Having acquired the knowledge for which he had striven so earnestly, Buddha decided to acquaint others with the true method of attaining spiritual deliverance. He commenced his public teachings in the "Deer Forest" near Benares, the first converts being the five ascetics of his exile. Others followed their example, and he soon obtained a large number of disciples, whom he despatched in all directions as missionaries to preach the new creed. The Buddhists gradually resolved themselves into two classes: the *Upasaka*, or laymen, who performed worldly duties, and the *Sramanas*, or ascetics, who strove for early admission into *Nirvana*.

There were five moral interdictions for both classes, namely :—

Do not take life; steal not; do not commit adultery; avoid lying; refrain from drinking strong liquor.

For the ascetics there were five more :—

Do not eat out of season; abstain from entertainments; do not use ornaments or perfumes; avoid comfortable beds; never receive gold or silver.

The virtues considered necessary for the gaining of the goal were charity, morality, patience, fortitude, meditation, and knowledge.

During a period of forty-four years Buddha preached throughout the tract now known as the United Provinces, and he died about 487 B.C., at the age of eighty, after having led a pious and exemplary life.

The great Emperor Asoka, who ruled over the greater part of India for more than forty years from 272 B.C., was responsible for the spread of Buddhism as a world-religion. When Gautama died, Buddhism was in its infancy, but Asoka established it as a State religion; he collected the literature then existing and put it into order; he held councils for the consideration of matters connected with the belief and arranged for the teaching of the doctrines throughout and beyond the limits of his great empire ; he had pious edicts engraven on rocks and pillars and in caves at numerous places in his dominions.

Another emperor, whose name is reverenced to this day in the legends of Tibet, Mongolia, and China, was Kanishka of the Kuchan dynasty, who for nearly thirty years from about 120 A.D. ruled over a large territory extending from Upper Sind into Central Asia, Tibet, and the west of China, and who reigned at Purushapura, the modern Peshawar. Kanishka followed Asoka's example in making Buddhism a State religion, and in the neighbourhood of his capital numerous traces of the religion are still found in the shape of ruined buildings, massive sculpture, and sacred relics.

Several reasons are given for the decline of Buddhism in India : it did not set itself to extinguish Brahmanism ; the celibacy of the monks was contrary to the instincts of the people ; the religion ignored the existence of God ; only those were assured salvation who elected to live as monks ; laymen were left in the cold and their duty was merely to attend to the wants of the clergy. The Hindus possessed a much more popular religion in Vishnuism and Sivaism, and those who had been converted to Buddhism gradually returned to the folds of the Brahmans, when it was declared that Buddha was an incarnation of Vishnu.

The Buddhist Scriptures.

There are two collections of ancient sacred books of Buddhism.

The best known are those preserved in Ceylon, called the *Tripitaka* (Three Baskets) from the manner in which the volumes were originally kept together. This collection, which is known as the "Lesser Vehicles" (*Hinayana*), was the result of a council of Buddhists held at Pataliputra on the Ganges under the direction of the Emperor Asoka; it is about twice the length of the Bible and is written in Pali. These documents are said to have been taken to Ceylon by Mahendra, the son of Asoka, when he visited that island as a religious mendicant and converted the people.

The first part, called *Vinaya-pitaka*, contains rules for the external life of the monks. The second, or *Sutta-pitaka*, consists of several works, each composed of short sayings or *sutras*, legends and stories about Buddha and others.

The third contains a number of disquisitions.

The most interesting of all these is the *Dhammapada*, or 'Path of Virtue,' for it is of exceptional literary merit and is believed to have been composed by Buddha himself.

The teachings of the *Hinayana* literature are followed by the Buddhists of Ceylon, Burma, and Siam.

The other collection of Buddhist scriptures is termed the *Mahayana*, or 'Greater Vehicle'; it consists of voluminous writings in Sanskrit, which some believe to have been brought together at a much later date than the Ceylon documents; stories regarding Buddha are introduced which have no place in the other books and indeed have a semblance to some of those in the New Testament. These books became the scriptures of the Buddhists of the north. The Tibetans, in the fifteenth century, adopted the organization of the Roman Catholic Church, with a pope, cardinal, prelate, bishops, abbots, priests, monks, and nuns; infant baptism, confirmation, investiture, masses for the dead, litanies, chants, rosaries, chaplets, candles, holy water, processions, saints' days, and fasts were all introduced.

In Tibet and Nepal there are a number of branches of the *Mahayana*, such as the *Bajrayana* (Thunderbolt School), *Sahajayana* (Easy School), *Mantrayana* (Mystic Formula School), and *Kala-chakrayana* (Sect of the Wheel of Time).

Modern Buddhism.

Nowadays Buddhism is perhaps seen at its best in Burma, where the people are taught by the monks to lead peaceable lives and to do good to their neighbours.

Every Burmese boy, who is not sent to a Government school, attends a monastery from the age of eight for a course of instruction in reading and writing and of general training in the precepts of Buddhism.

At the age of twelve or thereabouts he enters "holy orders" as a novice, this being effected by means of a ceremony like baptism, through which the youth receives a new name; clothes are discarded, his head is shaved, he recites certain prayers to receive admission to the "order," that he may achieve perfection and finally enter the holy state of *Nirvana*, or *Nehban* as it is called in Burma; he then receives yellow garments and a beggar's bowl from the head of the monastery, and the ceremonies conclude with a feast at the house of his parents.

The stay at one of these institutions is usually not longer than about six months if the novice intends to remain a layman; but, if he decides to lead a religious life, he has to enter upon a prolonged course of study of Buddhist literature.

In a Burmese monastery the daily routine is strict. The community is aroused shortly before daylight by the tolling of a large bell, and, after ablutions, each member recites a few formulas reflecting upon the goodness of Buddha in having revealed the method by which perfection can be attained and salvation thus secured.

After a slight meal, all the monks visit the neighbouring habitations in procession to receive doles of food in their bowls. On their return offerings are made to the image of Buddha and breakfast is then eaten. The day is taken up by ceremonial visits, the study of Buddhist writings and other work, meditation and the teaching of the novices.

Towards the end of the afternoon some of the monks and novices may take a stroll, but all must return to the monastery when the bell tolls at sunset; the day's work is then discussed, the younger members recite portions of what they have learnt to the abbot, and at about 8-30 P.M. all assemble for devotion before the image of Buddha; each member of the community then bows thrice before Buddha and before the abbot and retires.

A monk who has spent more than ten years in one of these institutions becomes qualified for appointment as a *Phon-gyee*, or person of 'great glory,' and from among these the *Sayah*, or abbot, is selected. Of yet higher rank than this is the Principal, who supervises a number of monasteries, and above these again are the eight *Sadaws*, or archbishops, who form a kind of supreme board for the control of all religious matters.

Discipline in the monasteries is strictly maintained, and offenders against the rules are punished by unfrocking, expulsion, and sometimes corporal punishment. Expelled monks are "put into Conventry," and have a very sorry time.

Monasteries are to be found attached to most of the larger villages in Burma. The monks, who are celibates, have great influence over the people, and in cases of evil living it is generally sufficient for them to show their displeasure by reversing their bowls when in procession, for the persons, against whom this disgrace is directed, to mend their ways.

One of the most wonderful groups of buildings in the world is the Royal Monastery outside Mandalay. Each part of it is intricately carved, and the whole is highly decorated with gilt and small pieces of looking-glass arranged in Mosaic fashion. Even the village monasteries are fine structures, and many of these buildings possess a richness of wooden carving which is unequalled in any other country.

The *Pagodas* are the churches of Burma; they are locally known as *Zaydee*, or the 'place of offering.' Each must contain a relic or some sacred object, such as a golden image of Buddha; they are generally constructed with domes, shaped like inverted bells; the spire on the top is usually capped by a *htee*, or umbrella. Here the public attend for prayer and on certain days—selected for each pagoda—there is feasting and merry-making, with illuminations in the evening. Sunday has become a holiday and festival in Lower Burma.

The building and maintenance of monasteries and pagodas are regarded as pious acts, and large sums are frequently spent on them and on the images of Buddha, which abound in every part of Burma.

The finest of the pagodas are the "Shway Dagohn Payah" at Rangoon, which is said to contain eight hairs and other relics of Gautama, and the temples at Mandalay, Pagahn, Pegu, Prome, and Shway Goo. On the steps of these may ordinarily be seen lepers, cripples, nuns in white robes, and others. who in plaintive tones call out for alms. During a festival the assemblage at the Shway Dagohn is well worth seeing, for the brightly dressed crowd of both sexes, gathered on and around the platform and steps of this magnificent edifice, forms, with its setting, a wonderful picture.

Buddhism was primarily intended to be free from idolatry, and in the monasteries the people are taught merely to repeat formulas and prayers for their own improvement ; they are not supposed to worship either images or relics, but there is little doubt that the masses actually worship Buddha and say their prayers and make their offerings to the material objects which they see before them.

Many of the more ignorant people actually ascribe miracles to particular images and others believe in *Nats*, or nature spirits, some of which are supposed to reside in the inferior heavens, like the Devas of the Vedic mythology, while some are believed to exist in the air, the water, and the forests.

The superstitions of the aboriginals still remain and exercise considerable influence over the masses in Burma, just as they do in India ; notwithstanding the teachings of the priests, demons and evil spirits are propitiated by the erection of little shrines, the making of offerings, the wearing of charms, and other practices.

In Burma there is no religious ceremony for marriage, and the monks are not called in to officiate as they are in Siam and in other Buddhist countries.

On the occasion of a death, however, it is otherwise; priests are then invited and they repeat prayers to drive away evil spirits and to purify the house; offerings are made to them and the corpse is thereafter cremated.

The obsequies of a monk are celebrated with great pomp, for on his death he is supposed to return to one of the heavens. The corpse of a *Phon-gyee* is enclosed in a gorgeous coffin and this is conveyed with much ceremony to a highly decorated structure, which is usually of enormous proportions and made of teak-wood, bamboo, cloth, and other materials; here the body lies in state for perhaps several months, while it is visited by large numbers of pilgrims, who make offerings of fruit, flowers, and money. Finally great quantities of combustibles are placed in the centre of the edifice and the whole is set on fire by means of fireworks in the presence of a large concourse. The ashes are collected and buried, but no tomb or shrine is erected over them.

Buddhism, in its Tibetan form, is still the religion of the people of Spiti in the east of the Kangra district. There it is practically free from Hinduism, but greatly impregnated with the indigenous demonology of the mountains. There are also a number of Buddhists in the neighbouring tract called Lahul.

The Tibetan *lamas*, or monks, are divided into three sects: the *Nyingpa*, who wear red garments and observe celibacy; the *Dokpa*, who also clothe themselves in red but are allowed to marry; and the *Gelukpa*, whose followers favour yellow caps and are celibates; the latter indulge in magic and incantations.

There are five monasteries in Spiti, of which four belong to the Gelukpa sect and one to the Dokpa. The Lahul lamas all belong to the latter sect, and the members of the sub-sect of these called *Sakyas* are held in some fear, for they practise magic and are generally weird people.

A large proportion of the male inhabitants of this territory receive education in Tibetan fashion in the monasteries, and some of the monks proceed to Lhasa for a religious training and take a sort of degree.

The sons of Dokpa lamas frequently become *buzhans*, or strolling friars, and small parties of these wander among the villages, obtaining a sustenance by acting, singing, and dancing. Their performances take the form of miracle-plays, which are acted in front of an image of their patron saint, behind which is scenery in the shape of a long screen, covered with quaintly painted pictures to illustrate the legends connected with their beliefs. Music is provided by means of conch shells, cymbals, and guitars; offerings of barley are thrown in the air and the crowd at intervals join with the performers in chanting the prayer *Om Mani Padme Hung*. The play comes to an end with a masque dance and wild gyrations on the part of the actors.

It may here be mentioned that there are six shapes in which souls may be reborn, namely:—Gods, Titans, Mankind, Beasts, Ghouls, and Hell;

in the prayer quoted above there are six syllables which represent these six kinds of existence and each of these has a special colour.

Om ....Gods .....White.
Ma ....Titans ...Blue.
Ni ....Mankind .Yellow.
Pad ....Beasts ...Green.
Me ....Ghouls....Red.
Hung ....Hell .....Black.

These colours are frequently used in the sacred banners, and sometimes the prayer is to be seen with each syllable painted in its distinctive colour. The prayer-wheels in the monasteries are also occasionally painted in this manner.

The interiors of the chapels attached to monasteries are elaborately decorated with frescoes of divinities, saints, and demons, and sometimes contain quaint pictures brought back from Lhasa by monks who have taken the degree of *gelong* there.

The *Dalai Lama,* or Pope of Lhasa, is held in the greatest respect by these people, for he is considered to be an incarnation of Buddha.

CHAPTER XIII.

JAINISM.

THE Jains are a sect, which arose out of Brahmanism by a religious movement probably founded in the sixth century B.C. by a *Jina* (spiritual conqueror) named Pārsvanāth. The religion, so formed, appears to have been reformed by Mahavira (great hero), a contemporary of Gautama Buddha; indeed the two religions of Jainism and Buddhism have much in common, which tends to show that they took their rise in the same age.

The Jains deny the divine origin and infallibility of the Veda; they reverence certain saints or holy mortals, who acquired, by self-denial and mortification, a status superior to that of the gods; and they lay great stress upon the preservation of animal life. They consider that the world is formed of eternal atoms and that it has existed and will exist eternally. They believe in an everlasting abode, where the soul, or *jiva* (meaning 'life'), is delivered from the necessity of transmigration, but it does not become absorbed in the universal spirit. No attention is paid by them to any Supreme God and they worship the saints, or *Jinas*, who sojourn in the blessed abode.

There are said to be twenty-four Jinas in each of three ages of enormous lengths; namely in the past, the present, and the future ages.

The twenty-four Jinas, or *Tirthankaras* as they are commonly termed, of the present age are as follows:—

No.	Name.	Place of birth.	Place of death.	Symbol.
1	Adi or Rishabha	Ayodhya ..	Gujerat.	Bull.
2	Ajita ..	Do. ..	Mt. Sikhar (Parasnath)	Elephant.
3	Sambhava ..	Sawanta ..	Do.	Horse.
4	Abhinandana	Ayodhya ..	Do.	Monkey.
5	Sumati ..	Do. ..	Do.	Curlew.
6	Padmaprabha	Kausambhi ..	Do.	Red Lotus.
7	Suparsva ..	Benares ..	Do.	Swastica.
8	Chandraprabha	Chandripur ..	Do.	Crescent.
9	Suvidha or Pushpadanta.	Kakendrapuri	Do.	Dolphin.
10	Sitala ..	Badalpur ..	Do.	Wishing Tree.
11	Sri Ansa ..	Sindh ..	Do.	Rhinoceros.
12	Vasupadya ..	Champapuri	Champapuri	Buffalo.
13	Vimala ..	Kumpalapuri	Mt. Sikhar	Boar.
14	Ananta ..	Ayodhya ..	Do.	Bear.
15	Dharma ..	Ratanpuri ..	Do.	Spiked Club.
16	Santa ..	Hastinapur	Do.	Deer.
17	Kunthu ..	Do. ..	Do.	Goat.
18	Ara ..	Do. ..	Do.	Fish.
19	Malli ..	Mithila ..	Do.	Water Vessel.
20	Muni-Suvrata	Rajgriha ..	Do.	Tortoise.
21	Nimi ..	Mithila ..	Do.	Blue Lotus.
22	Nemi ..	Dharika ..	Mt. Girinara	Conch.
23	Parsva ..	Benares ..	Mt. Sikhar	Serpent.
24	Mahavira or Vardhamana.	Chitrakot ..	Pawapuri	Lion.

To all of these names may be added the affix *Nath*, which is the Sanskrit for 'Lord'; thus Adi becomes Adinath and Parsva is known as Parsvanath.

The Jina is also termed *Jinesvara*, 'Chief of the Jinas'; *Arhat*, 'the Venerable'; *Tirthankar*, 'the Travelling Saint'; *Sarvajna*, 'Omniscient'; *Bhagavat*, 'the Holy One.'

In all Jain temples there are images of one or more of these Tirthankaras; before them the worshippers place candles, incense, and flowers; hymns of praise are chanted in their honour and pilgrimages made to spots sacred to their memory; in some places, on special days, the images are taken out in procession, being carried on highly decorated cars. Each of the Jinas has a separate animal, plant, or symbol, as his *chinha*, or sign; and these are given in the table above.

The existence of the Hindu gods is allowed, and some of these, which are connected with the legends of their saints, are admitted for worship in the Jain temples.

The principal of the Jinas are Parsvanath and Mahavira, the last two of the present age. Mahavira at first followed the teachings of his predecessor, but subsequently founded a separate order, the chief tenet of which was absolute nudity. After his death the Jain monks became divided into two sections; one of which retained the habit of nudity and became known as *Digambara* (sky-clad); the members of the other wore white garments and were called *Svetambaras* (clothed in white). Similarly their images were either nude or clothed.

The *Digambaras* of the present day wear coloured garments, and do not go naked except at meal times;

they are required to carry feathers from a peacock's tail in their hands.

The *Svetambaras* continue to wear white robes; they allow that the gentle sex can gain admission to the eternal abode, but the Digambaras deny this.

There are nowadays ascetic (*Yati*) as well as lay (*Sravaka*) Jains; the former are sometimes collected in *Pasala* (monasteries), but never officiate as priests in the temples, where the ceremonies are conducted by a layman, or by a Brahman trained for the purpose.

The *Yatis* carry brushes to sweep the ground before they tread or sit upon it; they use spiked shoes, wear cloth over their mouths and noses, and never eat nor drink in the dark; all of these customs being observed in order to avoid destruction of insect life. They wear their hair cut short, or plucked out from the roots, and practise continence and poverty. There are also female *Yatis*.

The Jains of the present day believe in nine *Tattva*, or 'truths.'

1. *Jiva*, or 'life,' consists of (*a*) animals, men, demons, and gods and (*b*) earth, water, air, fire, and the vegetable kingdom. Life has no beginning nor end; through sin it passes into animals; through virtue and vice combined it enters men; through virtue alone it enters the blessed abode.

2. *Ajīva*, or 'inaction,' comprises objects devoid of consciousness and life. Neither of these two can ever be destroyed, although their forms may vary.

3. *Punya*, or 'good,' is whatever causes happiness to living beings.

4. *Pāpa*, or 'ill,' is the cause of man's unhappiness.

5. *Asrava* is the source from which evil acts of living beings proceed.

6. *Samvara* is the cause by which acts are stored up or impeded.

7. *Nirgara* is the observance of penance for destruction of moral impurity.

8. *Bandha* is the association of life with acts.

9. *Moksha* is the liberation of the soul from the bonds of action; it means a profound calm or apathy but not annihilation. *Moksha* is obtained by "correct conduct" (*samyag-karitra*), "clear knowledge" (*samyag-jnāna*), and "right faith" (*samyag-darsāna*). For correct conduct the *Yati*, or Jaina ascetic, must keep his five vows, namely :—

1. Not to destroy life.
2. Not to lie.
3. Not to steal.
4. To be chaste and temperate in thought, word, and deed.
5. To desire nothing in this world immoderately.

For the laymen the rules are not so strict, but they must observe them to some extent; they are bound to be faithful to their wives and not to gain wealth by unfair means; they may not eat meat nor any other food, such as honey, involving destruction of animal life, and liquor must be avoided. Curiously enough they are forbidden to plough the earth, or even to cause others to do so, for this may involve injury to life.

Most of these regulations are followed somewhat strictly by Jains, with the result that the class, as a whole, is exceptionally well-behaved and they are most humane members of society. Caste is observed to a certain extent, but there is no general class reserved for priesthood, although they employ Brahmans sometimes. In the north and west of India Jains are mostly an educated class, engaged in commerce; in the south, notwithstanding the rule against ploughing, large numbers are agriculturists.

The principal Jain temples are remarkable for their elaborate structure and peculiar architecture.

The chief places of pilgrimage for Jains are situate in the midst of beautiful scenery on hill-sides and peaks.

Palitana, or the 'Abode of the Pali,' is the town at the foot of the sacred mountain Satrunjya (victorious over the foe), on which Jains from all over India have erected temples, small and large, sacred to Mahavira. The hill, which rises to a height of about 2,000 feet, is situated near the Gulf of Cambay in Kathiawar; it forms an abode of the gods, for it contains no habitations, save the rooms occupied by the priests and care-takers; some of the temples have large halls, the roofs of which are supported by carved columns, each of different design, and they are profusely ornamented in marble; all contain one or more marble figures of Mahavira, sitting with crossed feet like Buddha.

Mewar has, from remote times, afforded a refuge for the followers of the Jain faith, which was the religion of the people of Vallabhi, the first capital of the ancestors of the ruling chief. This State contains many Jain monuments and one of the most remarkable is a huge column, some 70 feet in height, dedicated to Parsvanath, in Chitor. There are also, at various places, large libraries of ancient Jain literature.

Mount Abu, in Rajputana, is another remarkable place of pilgrimage, and contains five temples, two being built wholly of marble, part of which is worked into most exquisite tracery and carving. In one of these there is a large statue of Parsvanath, and in all there are numerous figures of Mahavira.

Parasnath, a hill peak in Bengal, is the principal place of Jain worship in the east of India, and here, it is said, twenty of the Jinas entered into the divine abode, the last being Parsvanath, after whom the hill was named.

The temples at this place rise in tiers and form an unique picture in their dazzling whiteness. Their architecture is somewhat different from that of the Jain buildings in other parts of India, and seems to have borrowed from both Hindu temples and Muslim mosques.

The Jain scriptures are contained in different works, collectively called the *Siddhanta*, or 'Conclusion' (from the Sanskrit *siddha* 'proved,' and *anta* 'end'). These were brought together by Devarddhi about the sixth century A.D. at Vallabhi, the ancient capital of a State in Rajputana, which was sacked by Scythian invaders in 524 A.D. The works were probably composed about the end of the fourth and the beginning of the third centuries B.C. and, in the manner then usual in India, were repeated by word of mouth until they were finally recorded. Other older works, called *Purva*, are also said to have been in existence before these; but they were lost. The present books are partly in Sanskrit and partly in *Magadhi Prākrit.*

CHAPTER XIV.

SIKHISM.

Meaning of "Sikh."—The term *Sikh* means "disciple," and expresses the close dependence of this sect on their *Gurus* or 'teachers.' The name is directly obtained from the root of the Hindi word *sikhna*, 'to learn'; while *Guru* is a term derived from the Sanskrit root *gri*, 'to utter words.'

The Founder of Sikhism.—Sikhism (or Guruism as it might be called) was founded by a religious reformer named Nanak of the Bedi tribe, who was born at the village Talwandi, on the river Ravi near Lahore, in the year 1469 A.D.

Nanak's Predecessors.—Nanak was not the originator of an entirely new faith, but aimed at purifying the religions which he found existing in the Punjab. He based his teachings on those of his predecessors Jaidev, Ramanand, and Kabir, but especially upon the preachings of the latter.

Jaidev, the author of Gita Govind, taught, at the close of the twelfth century A.D., the worship of God alone in thought, word, and deed; sacrifices and austerities, he declared, were worth nothing compared with the repetition of God's name.

Ramanand founded, in the thirteenth century, sect of Hindus whose main idea was the worship of Vishnu under the form of Rama, hero of the

Ramayana, who is regarded by the great Hindu military races as their particular patron saint, or war-god, owing to his marvellous victory over the demon Ravana and his legions.

Kabir, whose sayings were constantly quoted by Nanak and his successors, was a weaver, who lived at Benares in the latter part of the fifteenth century. Although said to have been a Musalman by birth, he had no real sympathy with the Muslims and in the end became a pupil of Ramanand. He denounced idolatry, ridiculed the Shastras and Puranas, and taught Vaishnaism as a form of strict monotheism, with devotion to one god, called Vishnu, under such names as Rama and Hari; he, however, declared that the god of the Muslims was the same as that of the Hindus, and in this way attempted to bridge the gulf between Hinduism and Islam.

When Kabir died there was some difficulty regarding the disposal of his corpse, for both Hindus and Musalmans laid claim to it; while the wrangling was in progress he suddenly appeared and told them to look under the shroud; on doing so they found a heap of flowers—Kabir had disappeared. Thereupon the Hindus gathered up half the flowers and cremated them, and the Musalmans buried the remainder at Puri in Orissa, where a monastery was erected in his honour.

Guru Nanak.—Nanak taught his followers to believe in one God—neither Allah nor Ram, but simply God—the creator of the universe and of mankind and the God of all religions, God, devoid of fear, all-loving, unborn, immortal, self-existent, great, and bountiful. He rejected idols and incarnations, and maintained that all men were equal and there was no such thing as caste.

When Nanak was about to die he passed over his sons and nominated, as second Guru, his disciple Labana of the Trehan clan, whose name had been changed to Angada because of his "devotion." Thereafter two more were similarly appointed, and subsequently the succession became purely hereditary until the tenth and last Guru, Govind Singh.

The Ten Gurus.—The ten head Gurus of the Sikh religion were :—

1.	Nanak,	Bedi.	1469.
2.	Angada,	Trehan.	1539.
3.	Amar Das,	Bhalla.	1552.
4.	Ram Das,	Sodhi.	1574.
5.	Arjan,	do.	1581.
6.	Har Govind,	do.	1606.
7.	Har Rai,	do.	1645.
8.	Har Krishan,	do.	1661.
9.	Teg Bahadur,	do.	1664.
10.	Govind Singh,	do.	1675—1708.

The Sikh movement received a considerable impetus under the tolerant Emperor Akbar, who granted to Guru Baba Ram Das Sodhi, the land on which he excavated the large square lake called Amritsar (the Pool of Immortality). His son Guru Arjan, Sodhi, subsequently constructed the celebrated Golden Temple in the centre of this tank, and the large city, which has sprung up round this sacred spot, has since been regarded as the headquarters of the Sikhs. Guru Arjan is also distinguished as the compiler of the holy book, the *Adi Granth* (First Book), the materials for which he had received from his father. He established a system of tax-collecting from adherents of the faith and, after Akbar's death, incurred the displeasure of the Emperor Jehangir, who, considering that the Sikhs were gaining too much power, threw him into prison, where he shortly afterwards died.

The lives of the next three Gurus were comparatively uneventful, but the ninth Guru, Teg Bahadur, attracted the attention of the fanatical Emperor Aurangzeb, who summoned him to Delhi, where he was executed without reason in 1675. This act turned the Sikhs from a quiet reforming sect into a vigorous nation of fighting men under the tenth and last Guru, the warlike Sodhi Govind Singh, son of Teg Bahadur.

Guru Govind Singh called his followers *Khalsa* (from the Arabic *khalas*, 'pure') and directed them to attach the word *Singh*, or 'Lion,' to their names, so as to emphasize their military nature. He followed Nanak in teaching of the one god Vishnu, in rejecting caste and declaring equality among men, but he consolidated his people by introducing a ceremony of initiation and framing a set of regulations suitable for a military race.

The Five Signs.—Five outward signs were given to his followers in the following five Ks :—

1. *Kes*, uncut hair.
2. *Kachh*, drawers like "shorts."
3. *Kara*, an iron bangle.
4. *Khanda*, a two-edged knife or dagger.
5. *Khanga*, a comb.

He directed an occasional bath for purification in the holy lake at Amritsar and gave as a watch-word *Sri wah guru ji ka khālsa, Sri wah guru ji ki fatah*, which means '*khalsa* of God, victory to God.' The wearing of steel and the use of arms were ordered, while the use of tobacco in any form was prohibited.

Rite of Initiation.—The rite of initiation, which is called *Khānda ka Pāhul* (two-edged knife ceremony), consists of baptism with water in which sugar is dissolved; the mixture is stirred with the *khanda* and a portion is sipped five times by each new disciple, the remainder being sprinkled by five elders over five parts of the initiate's body, while he takes an oath not to mix with certain excommunicated persons, not to worship idols, to revere and bow to no one except a Sikh Guru, and never to turn his back on a foe. At the conclusion of the ceremony *karah parshad* (a mixture of flour, sugar, and ghee) is distributed to those present.

The *Pāhul* can be taken directly a boy arrives at years of discretion—about the age of seven—

but it is generally deferred until later. After initiation the five Ks must be worn and the name *Singh* used.

The Akalis.—After the death of Guru Govind Singh the Khalsa body is said to have been temporarily ruled by an ascetic named Bănda, but it subsequently fell under the direction of a military corporation of zealots, known as *Akāli*, or 'Faithful of the Eternal,' who became guardians of the sanctuary at Amritsar, where Guru Arjan's original "Granth" was preserved.

The *Akālis* were Sikh fanatics who aimed at carrying out the teachings of Guru Govind to the letter and even believed themselves justified in putting any opponent of their religion to the sword. They wore a blue uniform with a tall blue pugree, ornamented with steel quoits and other steel weapons, and they often went profusely armed, carrying sometimes as many as five swords. The five Ks were of course imperative.

These violent enthusiasts gave Ranjit Singh a considerable amount of tro ble, but he at length mastered them, and, nowadays, those who call themselves and dress as *Akālis* are few and far between and are mostly harmless individuals.

Relapse to Hinduism.—Except for respect paid to cows, other practices of the Hindus were practically abolished at the time of the tenth Guru, but since then there has been a tendency for Sikhs to join in Hindu festivals and ceremonies ; caste has to some extent been re-introduced, and nowadays some persons calling themselves "Singh" may only be distinguished from other Hindus by the fact that they refrain from the use of tobacco or wear the *kes*. Though the teaching of the Veda and Puranàs is reproved, the Brahman is still appointed as the family priest.

In the Report on the Census of the Punjab in 1901 Mr. Rose, in discussing the Sikh creed, gives the following summary :—

"It is not easy to say what is the distinctive creed of Sikhism. It is nearly always difficult to state a religious creed, and in the case of Sikhism there is the great difficulty that the Gurus from first to last strove, like the modern Hindu reformers, not to break away from the ancient beliefs, but to reconcile them with a purer creed. Unfortunately this resulted, as probably it always must result, in a medley of beliefs, so that within Sikhism we find many religious ideas at variance with its ideal creed. That creed involves belief in one God, condemning the worship of other deities; it prohibits idolatry, pilgrimages to the great shrines of Hinduism, faith in omens, charms, or witchcraft; and does not recognize ceremonial impurity at birth or death. As a social system it abolishes caste distinctions, and as a necessary consequence the Brahmanical supremacy and usage in all ceremonies, at birth, marriage, death, and so on. But this creed is probably accepted and acted up to by a very small number even of those who call themselves true Sikhs."

Sects.—It is difficult to classify the people who now call themselves "Sikh" into definite sects, but generally we may sort them into four divisions:—

1. The followers of Guru Nanak.
2. The disciples of Guru Govind Singh, known as *Kesdharis* (hair-wearers).
3. Persons who profess to follow one of the Gurus, or the claimants to the position of Guru.
4. Those who, while professing devotion to the tenets of one or more of the Gurus, and perhaps calling themselves "Singh," are almost indistinguishable from ordinary Hindus.

The **Udasis** are the genuine disciples of Nanak, and form a society of monks who reject the Granth of Govind Singh and accept only the Adi Granth. They were established by Dharma Chand, the eldest son of Nanak. They devote themselves to prayer and meditation and collect in monasteries under separate Gurus.

The Udasis are generally well dressed and do not solicit alms, while celibacy is not imperative. The initiation ceremony consists in the apprentice washing the great toes of five Udasis and then drinking the water so used; it is not surprising therefore that only a few of this sect now remain.

The **Kesdharis** include the Govind Singhis, the Hazuris, and Divane Sadhus.

The **Hazuris** are those Sikhs who have paid a visit to Hazur Sahib in Hyderabad, Deccan, where Guru Govind Singh died, and have been initiated there. The name is somewhat similar to the title of "Haji," which is given to a Musalman who has performed the "Haj" or pilgrimage to Mecca.

The **Govind Singhis** are the strict followers of the Guru from whom they take their name; they invariably wear the *kes* and generally the other four Ks, and they observe as far as possible the other restrictions ordained by their Guru.

The **Divane Sadhus** (Mad Saints) keep their hair long like the true Sikhs, and they go about in small parties, wearing few clothes; they favour necklaces of shells and carry a large feather for their head-dress.

The **Khalsa,** or *Tat Khalsa,* includes those who adhere to the command of Guru Govind Singh that the Granth is to be considered the Guru. The principal institution of this body is the Chief Khalsa Diwan, which has its headquarters at Amritsar with an elected committee and with branches in most parts of India, which are called "Khalsa Diwans" in important centres and "Singh Sabhas" in the smaller towns and villages.

The objects of this society are.

1. To work for the spiritual, intellectual, moral, social, and material betterment of the members.

2. To propagate the teachings of the Granth and of the *Guru Bani* (the ten Gurus' sayings).

3. To represent the claims of the Khalsa to Government.

This society has no connection with the management of the Golden Temple, except that the manager of that institution is ex-officio a member of their chief committee. They, however, regard that Temple as their Holy of Holies.

The **Nirmala Sadhus** (Pure Saints) observe celibacy and wear few clothes; they were formerly like Udasis, but they have now adopted reddish-yellow, instead of white robes, and are expounders of the Vedanta philosophy.

By far the greater number of persons calling themselves "Sikhs" have, at the latest census, not specified themselves as belonging to any particular sect, but they generally wear the *kes* and refrain from the use of tobacco.

The Sacred Books.

There are two holy books of the Sikhs. The Adi Granth (First Book) is the one mostly revered, and the *Dāsma Pādshād kā Grānth* (Book of the Tenth King) finds favour with the more fanatical section of the community.

The *Adi Granth* was compiled by Arjan, the fifth Guru, from materials collected and partly composed by his father. It is written in Gurmukhi and is divided into six parts:—

1. The *Japji* consists of verses by Nanak, used after the morning bath.
2. The *So Daru* is used at evening prayer.
3. The *So Purkhu*.
4. The *Sohila* is for use before going to sleep.
5. The *Rāg*, which are thirty-one in number, form the body of the book.

6. The *Bhog*, in thirteen chapters, is read at the various ceremonies.

The *Granth of the Tenth King* was composed by Govind Singh, the tenth and last Guru; it is written in Hindi, and forms a lengthy supplement to the Adi Granth, introducing the rules and regulations framed by its author.

The original *Granth*, which is also called "Granth Sahib," or "Darbar Sahib," is carefully treasured at Amritsar. During the daytime it is placed under a canopy in the Golden Temple and perpetually guarded by one of the "Granthees," or learned custodians of the holy book, and at night it is kept in a special iron-barred chamber at one side of the lake. It is the existing "Guru" of the Sikhs and as such is worshipped almost as a god.

CHAPTER XV.

ISLAM.

Islam is a faith which was introduced by the prophet Muhammad in the seventh century of the Christian era.

The term Islam is derived from the Arabic verb *salm* 'he was saved,' and means absolute resignation to the will of God; a follower thereof is called a *Muslim*, or *Musalman*.

In the second chapter (*Sura*) of the *Qoran*—the scripture of Islam—appears the following passage, which forms a concise summary of the chief principles of this religion :—

"It is not righteousness that ye turn your faces in prayer towards the east and the west, but righteousness is of him who believeth in God and the last day, and the angels, and the scriptures, and the prophets; who giveth money for God's sake unto his kindred, and unto orphans, and the needy, and the stranger, and those who ask, and for redemption of captives; who is constant at prayer, and giveth alms; and of those who perform their covenant, when they have covenanted, and who behave themselves patiently in adversity, and hardships, and in time of violence."

The five observances required of a Muslim are briefly :—

1. Belief that "there is no god but Allah (God) and Muhammad is the apostle of God."

2. Prayer (*Namaz*).

3. Fasting (*Roza*) during *Ramazan.*

4. Alms-giving (*Zukat*) to a tenth of their goods.

5. Pilgrimage to Mecca, once in a lifetime.

The first of these is the *Qalima,* or creed, of the Muslim. The Qalima, which is derived from various verses in the Qoran, consists of six sections :—*Taib, Shahādat, Tămjīd, Tauhīd, Istighfar,* and *Răd-i-Kufr.*

The *Taib* is *La-illaha-il-Ullaho—Muhammad ur-Rasul Ullah,* or 'There is no deity but God and Muhammad is the prophet of God.'

The *Shahādat* is "I testify there is no deity but God alone, without companion—and I testify that Muhammad is his servant and prophet."

Muhammad, who founded Islam, was the posthumous and only remaining son of one Abdulla of the Qoreish tribe, whose members were descended from Abraham through Ismael; his mother was Amina, daughter of a man called Wahab of the same tribe.

He was born at Mecca in 570 A.D., and shortly afterwards his grandfather took him to the *Qaaba*—then the chief temple of the Arabian idolaters—and there named him Muhammad, or the 'Praised One.'

After his grandfather's death, Muhammad, who was still young, was cared for by Abu Talib, one of his uncles, and, while in his charge, gained experience by accompanying him on a trading journey as far as Syria.

The young man received no education, but was observant and spent much time in meditation; he was given to wandering in the barren tract round about Mecca, and for a short period acted as a shepherd.

When he was twenty-five years of age, Khadija, a wealthy Qoreish widow, engaged him to take charge of a caravan, and he proceeded on a commercial journey to Bostra, not far from the Jordan in the direction of Damascus. After this excursion the couple fell in love with one another and shortly afterwards became man and wife. Khadija was a good woman, a loving companion, and an excellent mother, and, although she was much older than her husband, they lived together most happily, their only sorrow being the loss of their two sons in infancy.

As Muhammad advanced in years he showed signs of great intelligence and was frequently selected by the members of his tribe to decide religious and other disputes.

In the Qaaba there was a remarkable "Black Stone," which had always been held sacred by the Arabs. When the temple was being restored, a quarrel arose as to who should place it in its new position; Muhammad was called in and he settled the matter to everyone's satisfaction by putting a shawl underneath and directing the disputants to lift it together; they did so and Muhammad guided the stone into its resting place in the wall, where it is reverenced to this day.

At the age of forty Muhammad recommenced his solitary walks for the purpose of silent thought and, during these retirements, mused over the wickedness then prevalent among his Arab brethren; he sought for a means whereby idolatry might be abolished and injustice repressed, and, in their place, purity and righteousness installed.

It is related that one night in the month of Ramazan, when in a cave on Mount Hara near Mecca, the angel Gabriel came to him and revealed the fact that there was one God "Allah," and he, Muhammad, was the chosen Prophet of Allah. Other revelations are said to have followed, and Muhammad commenced to preach the doctrines, thus divinely communicated, to the people of Mecca.

Among the first converts to the new faith were his beloved wife Khadija, his friend Abu Bekr, whose daughter Ayesha he subsequently married, and Ali, who became his son-in-law. Several other relations and influential friends followed their example, and soon he obtained over a hundred adherents.

In 619 A.D. Khadija died, and a few months later he married Ayesha and thereafter took to himself a number of wives, in accordance with the custom which was then common among the Arabs.

From time to time, as he needed advice, further revelations were vouchsafed to him, and Muhammad had these recorded by those of his companions who were literate.

As might be expected, the new faith met with much opposition, and the followers became subject to persecution by their tribesmen ; in 622 A.D. this reached such a pitch that most of them found it expedient to leave Mecca and move to Medina (Yathreb), where they were well received. Shortly afterwards Muhammad, against whom plots had been hatching, was also compelled to depart. He left secretly with his faithful companion Abu Bekr on the night of the 15th July, and, after a few months spent in wandering, they made a triumphant entry into Medina, where they joined their friends.

This departure is called the *Hijra*, or 'Flight,' and the Muslim era commences from the day after it.

At Medina the first mosque was built and services were started. After a time the number of followers greatly increased, and Muhammad, already the Prophet of God, became high priest, chief magistrate, and, finally, ruler of the people.

In accordance with the divine instructions, received through the angel Gabriel, the Prophet now brought together an army and commenced a holy war against idolaters and disbelievers. The famous centre of Mecca fell into his possession early in 630 A.D., that is, in the eighth year after the "Flight"; the idols in the Qaaba were immediately destroyed, and this famous temple was converted into a mosque.

After considerable fighting Muhammad consolidated his dominions which, in the course of ten years, had grown into an empire.

At the age of sixty-two the Prophet felt his end drawing near, but he continued to lead the prayers in the mosque at Medina until compelled to take to his bed. During this final illness he expressed a desire to be interred at Medina, which had given the faith such a noble reception. He had long previously given out that he was merely a man, and he now exhorted the people not to make his tomb an object of worship. The last words to fall from the lips of this remarkable man were: "Pardon me, O God, and unite me to the blessed companionship on high."

The death of the great leader caused a commotion in the land, and it became necessary to appoint a Khalifa, or successor, without delay. Muhammad left no son as heir, and it was not the custom for a daughter to succeed to a chiefship; he had given no instructions on the subject, but during his last days had deputed Abu Bekr to lead the people at prayers, and after considerable dissension the choice fell upon this man, the best of his friends.

It was this dispute which led to the division of the Prophet's followers into two distinct factions; for there were those who regarded Abu Bekr, with his successors Omar and Osman, as usurpers and considered that Ali, the cousin and son-in-law of Muhammad, should have been appointed on the Prophet's death and that one of Ali's sons Hassan and Hossain should have followed him.

Ali subsequently came to the Khalifate, but this did not mend matters.

Before the end of the seventh century the Musalmans had spread abroad and carried their faith into the north of Africa and part of Central Asia.

Islam was introduced into India in the eighth century A.D. from the north-west; thereafter successive waves of Muslim invasions rolled into the country from the same direction until the latter half of the eighteenth century. The conquerors forced their religion upon the people; it obtained a great hold in the north of India—from Sindh and the Punjab in the west to Bengal in the east—but it did not influence so much the more southerly states, which, for the most part, have remained Hindu.

Many of the Indian converts to Islam continued to follow the customs pertaining to their original faith, and we even find Muslim families which bear both Hindu and Muslim names. On the other hand, the invaders adopted many of the Hindu manners.

Thus the habits of Musalmans in India differ considerably from those of their confrères in Arabia, Persia, Turkey, Egypt, and elsewhere. The converts moreover retained, and the new-comers acquired, many of the superstitions of the countryside. It is indeed not an unheard of occurrence for a Muslim yokel in an Indian village to make offerings for the appeasement of one of the Hindu deities. As a general rule, however, the main principles of Islam have retained their purity in India.

CHAPTER XVI.

THE QORAN AND ITS DOCTRINES.

THE gospel of Islam is the *Qoran*, which means 'that which ought to be read'; it is always termed *Qoran Sherif*, or 'Holy Qoran,' by Muslims.

The faithful believe that it was sent down by God during the night of *al Qadr* into the lowest heaven, whence it was revealed in portions to Muhammad, as occasion required, by the Angel Gabriel. There is some doubt as to the exact date of this night, but most Muslims believe it to have been one in Ramazan and probably that which falls between the 26th and 27th of this month.

The communications thus made were recited by the Prophet and written by any literate follower, who happened to be present, on palm leaves, pieces of wood, and such like fragments. After Muhammad's death, the various documents were collected, arranged, and copied out.

In 650 A.D. the Khalif Osman had an authoritative text prepared and all others were destroyed, so the Qoran now retains very much the same form as that in which it was prepared within nineteen years of the death of Muhammad.

The book is divided into one hundred and fourteen *suras*, or chapters, each of which is known, not by a number but by a title derived from some important matter dealt with, or by a particular word mentioned therein; sometimes the name consists of one or more initial letters, the meanings of which are often obscure. It is written in Arabic with extreme elegance and purity of language, and is regarded by all Muslims as miraculous, inimitable, and infinitely sacred.

Muhammad believed that his mission was to restore the ancient religion of Abraham, ancestor of the Qoreish tribe; the essence of the Qoran therefore is the "unity of God." He taught that prophets were sent by God to lead the people into the right way whenever they became corrupt, or neglected the true faith.

Many of the historical facts of the Old Testament are repeated in the Qoran, and numerous traditions, which were prevalent in the days of Muhammad, are introduced; a great deal of the book is taken up with instructions as to right conduct in daily life and especially as to the worship of the one true God; there are also a number of passages explaining circumstances, or events, which happened during the lifetime of the Prophet, including his own actions.

Islam may thus be said to consist of two distinct parts, namely, *Iman* or 'Faith,' and *Din* or 'Practice.'

To have faith, a true Muslim must not only believe in the one God and his absolute power, but also in his angels, his prophets, his scripture, in the resurrection, and in the day of judgment.

Among the prophets, of whom there were many thousands, the seven of most importance were

Adam, Noah (*Nooh*), Abraham (*Ibrahim*), Moses (*Musa*), David (*Daud*), Jesus (*Isa*), and Muhammad; the latter being the greatest of all.

Musalmans believe that at death an angel separates the soul from the body and conveys it to one of the heavens. The soul of a prophet proceeds direct to paradise; that of a martyr to another comfortable place of green pastures; and there is a difference of opinion regarding the disposal of the spirit of an ordinary believer; some think that it remains in a state of rest near the sepulchre, others hold that it stays with Adam in the lowest heaven or near the throne of God, and there are yet others who believe that it resides in the sacred well Zam-Zam at Mecca, the waters of which were considered holy from ancient times.

As for the souls of the wicked and of disbelievers, they are thrust into hell to receive torment.

The general opinion regarding the day of judgment is that the soul will rejoin the body and all mankind will be called upon to account for their actions. At the conclusion of the great trial all will pass over a bridge (*sirat*), and those who have done well will enter paradise (*Jannat*), and those who have done evil will fall headlong into *Jehennam*, or into one of the six other compartments of hell.

Muslims are taught that there is a devil named Satan, who uses his influence to lead persons astray, and yet they believe in predestination.

The Qoran enters into long descriptions of the glory and felicity of paradise; this heavenly abode possesses, among other comforts, cool rivers flowing with sparkling water, milk, wine, and honey; unlimited wine can be imbibed there without evil effect; in its gorgeous palaces are celestial black-eyed houris of perfect shape and strict modesty, who will wait upon and delight the faithful; perpetual youth will be enjoyed, and there will be no distinction in the treatment of the sexes. Large numbers of Muslims no doubt accept these words in their literal sense, but the more thoughtful receive them as having an allegorical meaning; just as Christians regard the very similar description of paradise contained in the hymn "There is a land of pure delight."

Women are given a much higher status in the Qoran than they held in Arabia prior to the teaching of the Prophet. It enables them to possess, deal with, and inherit property; it enjoins their kind treatment and declares that they are equal with men as regards religious duties and ultimate bliss. Muhammad's first wife Khadija and his daughter Fatima were evidently model women in tehir day, and he is said to have remarked of them that they "attained perfection."

In an interesting article entitled "The Influence of Women in Islam," which appeared in the *Nineteenth Century*, (May 1899), Syed Ameer Ali writes: "When the woman stands by the side of the husband possessed of full rights, with a free independent will, not merely the mother of his children but the mistress of the household, not a simple toy but a comrade and friend, only then can it be said that the people among whom the relations of thetwo sexes are thus developed are a truly cultured race." Of Fatima he says: "She had received an education which placed her on a par with most of the educated men in her country. Her character was one of unmingled sweetness and gravity, which deepened as she grew older .... She lectured to mixed congregations of both sexes often in the courtyard of her house, and sometimes in the public mosque. Many of her sermons are still extant."

It is difficult to understand how the strict *pardah* system, now in vogue among Muslims in India, came into force. Why is it that nowadays women are not admitted into the mosques for worship? Why are they shut up in *zenanas*, or harems, and practically cut off from all intercourse with their fellow-beings? Such a procedure is certainly not inculcated in the Qoran, for in the chapter entitled "Light" we read: "And speak unto the believing women, that they restrain their eyes, and preserve their modesty, and discover not their ornaments, except what necessarily appeareth thereof; and let them throw their veils over their bosoms, and not show their ornaments, unless to their husbands, and let them not make a noise with their feet, that their ornaments which they hide may thereby be discovered." The directions contained in this passage would be entirely unnecessary if women were bound to remain in *pardah*, and there is nothing in the Qoran, except as regards the Prophet's own wives, which prohibits the appearance of women in public, or restrains them from showing their faces.

Apparently the origin of this dreadful ban upon the weaker sex is due to an edict issued by Qadir, the Abbaside, which forbade women to enter mosques or colleges, or to appear in public without the *burka*, and, as Syed Ameer Ali says, "With that commenced the decadence of Islam."

The Qoran permits a man to have as many as four wives at a time, provided they are equally treated and loved by the husband; the actual words of the Qoran are, "If you are afraid you cannot do justice to all, then have only one," so a man must also have sufficient means to support them; it prohibits marriage within certain degrees of relationship. No special rite is laid down for marriage, but in India it is customary for a *nikah khwan*, or marriage-reader, who is usually a *maulvi*, to attend and, in the presence of the betrothed couple and several other witnesses, to read a few verses from the Qoran, after ascertaining that the parties consent to the ceremony.

At the age of puberty Musalman girls have the right to repudiate betrothals entered into previously, but, being under control, they seldom exercise it.

Widows may not marry again until four months and ten days have passed and, if pregnant, must wait until delivered.

Divorce of a wife by a husband is permitted, even on grounds of dislike, and is effected by his merely saying, " Thou art divorced " ; but a woman can only claim a divorce in very exceptional circumstances. The husband is directed to provide necessaries for a divorced wife for the period of *iddat, i.e.*, three lunar months after divorce, and he may remarry her, but after divorcing one three times may not marry her again, unless in the meantime she has married and been divorced from someone else or has become a widow.

There are many vices which are inveighed against in the Qoran, and from some of these, such as gaming and drinking, the majority of Muslims are remarkably free. In the chapter entitled " The Table " it is written : " O true believers, surely wine and lots, and images and divining arrows, are an abomination of the work of Satan ; therefore avoid them, that ye may prosper." The pious Muslim does not play any game of chance ; he is fond of chess, or any game in which skill alone is required, but the pieces used must be plain ones and not in the form of figures. The commandment " Make not to thyself any graven image " is taken literally by Muslims, who, in their art, restrict themselves to plant life and geometrical designs, avoiding shapes of animals.

Regarding money-lending it is declared that " Whatever ye shall give in usury, to be an increase of men's substance, shall not be increased by the blessing of God " and " They who devour usury shall not arise from the dead." Muslims therefore do not as a rule take interest or invest money.

Cheating is dealt with in the eleventh chapter by the passage: " O my people, give full measure, and just weight ; and diminish not unto men aught of their matters ; neither commit injustice in the earth, acting corruptly. The residue which shall remain unto you as the gift of God, after ye shall have done justice to others, will be better for you, than wealth gotten by fraud, if ye be true believers."

Prayer is strictly enjoined throughout the Qoran, from which the following passages may be quoted :—

" Celebrate the praise of thy Lord before the rising of the sun and before the setting thereof, and praise him in the hours of the night and in the extremities of the day that thou mayest be well pleased with the prospect of receiving favour from God." (*Sura* entitled " T.H.")

" Rehearse that which hath been revealed unto thee of the book of the Qoran : and be constant at prayer, for prayer preserveth a man from filthy crimes, and from that which is blameable : and the remembering of God is surely a most important duty." (*Sura* entitled " The Spider. ")

In accordance with tradition there is a complicated ritual for worship at the mosque and for daily prayer wherever a Musalman may be. The five times for saying prayers are :—

1. At dawn and before sunrise.

2. From the decline of the sun to the equalling of the shadow.

3. From the equalling of the shadow to sunset.

4. From sunset to darkening of the night.

5. From the darkening of the night to dawn.

Prayers at the "Id"—a festival which will be described in the next chapter—are said between the rising of the sun and noon, and it is customary for a sermon to be preached after this service and before the Friday mid-day prayers.

The faithful are summoned to prayer by the *muazzim*, or "caller," who is specially appointed for the purpose at large mosques, or by the *mullah* or *maulvi* of the smaller or village *masjids*. The *azan*, or "call," is pronounced in a solemn resounding tone and is as follows :—

"God is great (four times), I testify that Muhammad is the apostle of God (twice), Come to the prayer (twice), Come to the blessing (twice), God is great (twice). There is no god but God." In the morning are added the words "Prayer is better than sleep (twice)."

Public prayers are led by an *imam*, *mullah*, or one of the assembled worshippers and all prayers consist of a series of *rakaats*, or forms of prayer, which are repeated in a variety of devout positions.

Before saying prayers and taking food, the faithful are required by their scripture to wash their faces and hands and their arms up to the elbows; also to rub their heads and feet and to put on clean clothes.

In cases of pollution the body must be washed all over; also before Friday prayers, the great festivals, and after washing the dead. If water is not forthcoming, fine sand may be used instead. These appear to be the only hygienic rules prescribed by the Qoran; it makes no mention of the sanitation of dwelling places and their surroundings, nor does it refer to medical treatment or to precautions necessary during epidemics.

A Muslim repeats "*Bismillah*" (In the name of God) before a meal, and on finishing says "Glory to God." Eating of blood and the flesh of swine is prohibited, also whatever dies of itself, or is slain in honour of an idol, or is strangled, killed by a blow or fall, or by another beast. Animals, other than pigs, may be killed by mankind for the purpose of food, but no game may be killed during a pilgrimage; fish, however, may be caught then for supply. Animals or birds killed by others which have been trained to do so, such as birds or hares caught by hawks, may be eaten.

No special method of taking the life of an animal seems to be mentioned in the Qoran, but a practice called *halal* has arisen. The literal meaning of this word is 'lawful,' but it has come to imply the method of slaying an animal to be used for food by cutting its throat, and a strict Muslim only eats the flesh of those slaughtered in this manner. The idea is that the blood is removed by this process.

When a Musalman is dying, a *mullah*, or a skilled reader of the Qoran, is sent for, and he reads the thirty-sixth chapter entitled "Y.S." a portion of which runs :—" It shall be but one sound of the trumpet, and behold, they shall be all assembled before us. On this day no soul shall be unjustly treated in the least; neither shall ye be rewarded but according to what ye shall have wrought. On this day the inhabitants of paradise shall be wholly taken up with joy: they and their wives shall rest in shady groves, leaning on magnificent couches. There they shall have fruit, and they shall obtain whatever they shall desire. Peace shall be the word spoken unto the righteous, by a merciful Lord: but he shall say unto the wicked: 'Be ye separated this day, O ye wicked, from the righteous. Did I not command you, O sons of Adam, that ye should not worship Satan, because he was an open enemy unto you? And did I not say: worship me, this is the right way?"

The burial service is read by a *mullah* in a *mosque* or *masjid*, or in some open space, and it concludes by his saying, "It is the decree of God," to which the chief mourner replies, "I am pleased with the will of God," and then intimates that the people attending may depart.

The corpse is placed on its back in the grave, the head to the north and twisted to the right, so that the face is towards Mecca.

The following words end the ceremony :—" We commit thee to earth in the name of God, and in the religion of the Prophet."

On the third day after the burial it is customary for relatives to visit the grave, by which a *mullah* recites portions of the Qoran.

Above the actual grave is placed a simple oblong monument of cement or stone, that for a man being slightly different from the one for a woman; over this is sometimes built a tomb of elaborate design. The *Taj Mahal* at Agra is perhaps the most beautiful mausoleum in the world; it was erected by the Emperor Shah Jehan over the remains of his queen Mumtaz Mahal (Exalted of the Palace).

CHAPTER XVII.

MUSLIM FESTIVALS AND FASTS.

THE dates for festivals and fasts observed by Muslims are regulated by their calendar.

The Muslim era dates from the 16th July, 622 A.D., *i.e.*, the day after Muhammad's flight (*hijra*) from Mecca. The years are purely lunar and therefore get behind the solar calendar, making a complete cycle in about 32½ years. This circumstance has to be remembered in India, for it happens occasionally that certain Hindu and Muslim festivals fall upon the same day and special arrangements have to be made to prevent the clashing of religious processions of the two different creeds. Another point to be remembered is that the date of a festival may be retarded for a day or so, owing to the new moon being obscured by clouds.

The names of the Muslim months and principal festivals are given on the next page.

Months.	Number of days.	Festivals.	Dates.
1. Muharram	30	Muharram	1st to 10th.
2. Săphăr	29		
3. Răbi-ul-āwăl	30	Băra Wafāt	12th.
4. Răbi-ul-sāni	29	Husain's birthday. ..	
5. Jamada-ul-āwăl	30		
6. Jamada-ul-sāni	29		
7. Răjăb	30	Day of Victory	15th.
		Prophet's ascension ..	20th.
8. Shābān	29	Shăb-i-Barāt	14th
9. Rămăzān	30	Fast of Rămăzān	1st to 30th.
10. Shāwūl	29	Rămăzān Id or Id-ul-Fitr ..	1st or day after new moon is seen.
11. Dhul-qāda (zul-qād) ..	30	..	
12. Dhul-hija (zil-hăj) ..	29 or 30	Bakr-Id or Id-ul-Zuha ..	10th.

The Muharram. The Muslim month of mourning is called Muharram, the first month of their year. New Year's Day with the Musalmans dawns as a day of grief and lamentation, for it is the prelude to the greatest tragedy in Islam. The fateful tenth of the month is the anniversary of the martyrdom of Husain, the son of Ali and grandson of the Prophet. On that day occurred the massacre at Kerbala.

Ali was the fourth Khalif of Islam; on his death a general named Moaviah installed himself in his place, and when he died his son Yazeed was appointed successor. The people appealed to Imam Husain at Mecca to free them from the intolerable yoke of Yazeed, and he started with a party, consisting of his family and a few devoted followers, for Kufa. On the way he encamped at Kerbala near the banks of the Euphrates, and there he was surrounded. After a conference, fighting began and Husain with his party were all slaughtered.

In Shiah homes, in apartments called *Imambara* or *Husain Dalan*, ceremonies are performed in this connection; these are on a large scale at Hyderabad, Bombay, Lucknow, Dacca, Murshidabad, Patna, Hooghly, and Calcutta, where the Shiahs predominate.

In Persia—the centre and stronghold of Shiaism —the event is commemorated with great pomp and solemnity in buildings called *Takya*.

The *imambara* is decorated profusely with flags and shawls, professional reciters discourse on the episodes of the tragedy, the audience weep copiously; there are lamentations and beating of the breasts with hands and sometimes self-scourging with iron chains and other instruments.

The more important *majlis* (assemblies) are held at the principal *imambaras*. On the 7th, 8th, and 10th of Muharram processions are formed to represent the three battles fought on those dates. These are headed by a large glass case called *Zulfakar*, containing the imaginary sword of Husain and other sacred articles. Persons follow with silver-handled flags and poles surmounted with cones or hands—the *allam*, or standard, of Imam Husain was of green colour with a five-finger design upon it. They march in solemn silence. At the rear are led a number of richly caparisoned horses with turbans and swords on their backs; milk is sprinkled on the horses' feet by the public. These animals are called *Dulduls*, and represent the steeds of the Imam. Large groups of mourners accompany them, reciting verses and beating their chests. This portion of the procession represents the battle-field of Kerbala.

Only Shiahs take out the *Duldul* at Muharram, and where they are few this portion of the ceremony is generally not allowed as it leads to ill-feeling *Duldul* was the name of the horse on which Husain rode and which returned riderless when its master was slain.

The tenth of the month is the *ashura*, or special, day, and the procession is then followed by an imitation funeral cortege. The *Sunnis* then bring out a number of *tazias*, which are imitation shrines made of paper, pith, and tinsel on a framework of bamboo; some are small and carried by one person, others are so large that they require a dozen or more men to carry them.

Price Collier, in his book "The West in the East," thus describes this part of the ceremony as performed at Lucknow :—"Various features of the tragic history of the death of Hassan and Husain are represented during the procession and at the interment; and every now and again the procession halted, while an excited orator rehearsed some portion of the story. They marched, shouting the names of the martyrs, beating their breasts, throwing dust on their heads; they are all bare-headed on this occasion, weeping and wailing. One group carried what looked like short flails and to the end of the cords were tied knife-blades; these they whirled around their heads, bringing them down on their shoulders and backs, which were streaming with blood.

To see a group of these men stop and burst into groans, tears, and wild cries of grief; to see their breasts bruised and in some cases the skin broken by the beating of their fists; to see them covered with blood, dust, and sweat, their faces haggard, their eyes blazing with excitement; to hear one of them recite part of the tale of woe, his eyes streaming with tears and his voice choked with emotion; and the tale punctuated with wild cries and shrieks and lusty pummelling of the breast on the part of his hearers, while little children and old women threw dust on their own and each other's heads, is the most amazing spectacle of religious enthusiasm that one may see anywhere in the world to-day."

The chief difference in the observance of the Muharram is that the Shiahs celebrate it with mourning and bring out *Dulduls*, whereas the Sunnis do not.

During this fatal month of Muharram the Khalif Osman was assassinated in 656 A.D., Ali was stabbed to death in a mosque at Kufa in 660 A.D., Hassan was poisoned during his retirement in a hermitage near Medina, and last of all Husain was speared to death in the conflict at Kerbala by a man named Shamir, a name which is detested by Shiahs to this day.

Akhiri Chahar Shambah (Last fourth day after Sabbath). The last Wednesday of Sãphãr is observed in some places as a festival in commemoration of the mitigation of Muhammad's last illness and his last bath.

Bara Wafat means the 'Great Death' of the Prophet ; it is observed as a solemn festival on the 12th of Răbi-ul-āwăl, which was also the day of his birth.

Shab-i-Barat, or 'Night of Record,' is the night of the 14th of Shābān when God is said to register all actions of mankind and all births and deaths for the coming year ; it was originally set apart for fasting, but has become a festival and a great day for fireworks; in the north of India lamps are lighted at graves and shrines and prayers are said on behalf of deceased ancestors.

Ramazan. The fast of Rămăzān is strictly observed by all Muslims. During its thirty days, between dawn and sunset, they eat nothing, drink nothing, and smoke nothing. Owing to the months not following the seasons it happens that this month falls in the hot weather during many years in succession, and the privation then endured may be imagined when it is remembered that the temperature in the shade during the day-time in India is frequently above 100° Fahrenheit.

The fast must be especially trying to Muslim servants, who have to cook and serve the meals of their European employers.

Those who are sick or on a journey are especially excused from fasting and must afterwards make up the days so lost; but pregnant women, and those who are nursing or in their courses, and young children, are entirely exempt.

Id-ul-Fitr, or feast of breaking the fast, begins on the first day of Shāwūl and continues for two days. The new moon, however, must be seen on the last evening of Rămăzān, and, if it is not, the fast has to be prolonged until a view is obtained. It is naturally looked forward to and celebrated with great rejoicing by the Muslims, who then make amends, as it were, for the mortification of the preceding thirty days. On the morning of the *Id* all good Muslims perform careful ablutions, put on spotless white clothes—gorgeous raiment for the worship of God is forbidden—and distribute alms. Towards ten o'clock they gather at the *id-gah*, a large enclosure outside the habitations, where a special service takes place until nearly noon. Afterwards the people greet one another much as do Christians at Christmas time, and they spend the remainder of the day in feasting and rejoicing.

Id-ul-Zuha or 'feast of daylight,' **Bakr-Id** or 'goat festival,' *Id-ul-Kurban* or 'feast of sacrifice,' and *Id-ul-Kabir* or 'great festival,' are all held on the 10th of Dhul-hija. The festival is usually termed *Bakr-Id* and is in memory of the sacrifice of a ram or goat in lieu of his son by Abraham. In the Qoran it is not definitely stated whether it was Ismael or Isaac who was to be offered, but most Muslims believe it to have been Ismael, for the wording shows that only one son was alive at the time and the promise of Isaac is mentioned in a subsequent verse; some believe that both sons were offered at different times.

The incident is commemorated every year by the sacrifice of rams or goats at the *masjids* or *id-gahs*, and in large cities there is a considerable sale of the sacrificial animals on the evening before the festival.

The Sacred Months. Four months were held sacred by the pagan Arabs, namely, Răjăb, Dhul-qāda, Dhul-hija, and Muharram. Dhul-hija was the month for the performance of a pilgrimage to

Mecca, and, in order to allow time for the journey to and fro, the preceding and following months were also kept free. During this period it was unlawful to wage war; the people laid aside their arms, blood feuds were stayed, and no matter how bitter the hatred, enemies observed a holy truce. The month of Răjăb was kept sacred in the same manner and was observed as a fast. When Muhammad commenced his preachings it was deemed desirable to continue the practice of the pilgrimage and to keep holy the three months of Dhul-qāḍa, Dhul-hija, and Muharram, but in lieu of Răjăb the month Rāmăzān or Rămădān, which had formerly been a time for excessive drinking, was selected for fasting and because, as the sacred book itself records, it was the month in which the Qoran was sent down from heaven.

The Hajj, or *Hadj*, is the pilgrimage to the temple at Mecca which every Muslim, who has health and sufficient means, should perform at least once in his lifetime. Pilgrims have to be present at Mecca at the beginning of the month Dhul-hija; those from India proceed by sea to Jedda and at that place don their sacred clothes (*ihram*) which only consist of two small woollen clothes and a pair of sandals which expose the heel and instep; bare-headed and thus clad they walk to the holy city and during the pilgrimage must be most particular in their language and manners.

The temple at Mecca consists of several enclosures in the centre of which stands the *Kaaba*, the holy of holies; round this edifice the pilgrims must proceed in a special manner seven times, commencing at the corner where the black stone, previously mentioned, is fixed; on each occasion as the stone is passed they either kiss it or touch it with their hand and kiss that. During the first nine days of Dhul-hija there is a series of ceremonies to perform, including visits to certain sacred spots in the enclosure and other holy places in the immediate neighbourhood of Mecca.

Muslims believe that the well *Zam Zam*, close by the Kaaba, is the identical spring which gave water for Ismael when wandering with his mother Hagar in the desert, and some think that she called out *zam zam* or 'stop stop,' on finding it. The water is regarded as exceptionally holy; it is drunk with special devotion by the pilgrims who fill bottles and carry it away.

The Black Stone is an object of great reverence; it is set in silver and rests in the south-eastern corner of the Kaaba. It is considered to have been sent down to the earth from heaven with Adam and placed in the Kaaba by Abraham when he was constructing this edifice. In the enclosure there is another sacred stone on which Abraham is said to have stood when he was giving directions for the building.

All the ceremonies now performed during the pilgrimage were observed by the Arab idolaters prior to the time of Muhammad, and the only difference is that the idols do not remain.

Friday is the day of the week established for special worship by Muslims; it was probably so set apart because the people had been accustomed to assemble then to discuss tribal and other matters. No special reason is given in the Qoran for its selection, but advice is given to leave merchandizing and sport on that day. Tradition says that it was sanctified because the Prophet made his first entry into Medina and God finished creation on Friday.

All festivals are observed by alms-giving and extra prayer at the *masjids* or at the *id-gah*.

CHAPTER XVIII.

ISLAMIC SECTS, SAINTS, AND SUPERSTITIONS.

Sects.

ISLAM has been divided into sects almost from the day of the Prophet's death, and Muhammad himself prophesied a split among his followers when he announced :—

"The Magians are sub-divided into seventy sects, the Jews into seventy-one, the Christians into seventy-two, and in my religion there will be seventy-three, all of which, except one, will enter the fire and perish." There are now probably considerably over a hundred distinct religious parties among Muslims, but the two principal divisions are the *Sunnis* and the *Shiahs*, the former being by far the most numerous in India and the latter being found in scattered communities except in certain well-known centres, such as Lucknow. Both contain a number of sub-sects.

The Sunnis form the orthodox section of Islam and believe in the *Sunnah*, or 'tradition' of the Prophet from which they derive their name, as the canonical authority. They consider that the people had the liberty to elect the successors to the Khalifate and thus uphold the succession of Abu Bekr, Omar, and Osman to this position.

They accuse the Shiahs of having corrupted the Qoran and of not following its precepts.

The Shiahs (a name derived from *Shihat* meaning 'followers'), or *Adliyah* (rightful society) as they call themselves, reject the Sunnah as having been compiled under the direction of the three Khalifs above mentioned, whom they regard as usurpers. They claim for the descendants of Muhammad hereditary right to the Khalifate and hold that only Ali and his line should have followed the Prophet as leader, or *Imam* of the faithful.

Ali was not only the Prophet's cousin but the husband of Fatima, the only surviving daughter of Muhammad by Khadija.

The Shiahs show great hatred for the three earlier Khalifs and maltreat their effigies on the occasion of a festival called *Ghadir*, so named from the place in Arabia where Muhammad is said to have declared Ali as his rightful successor.

Ali is venerated by them equally with Muhammad, and they add to the creed "and Ali is the Wali (agent or confidant) of God."

They further believe in what is called *Nur-i-Muhammad*, 'the light of Muhammad,' which is supposed to have passed to Ali and then to the "twelve Imams" (*Imambara*). The last of these, who disappeared in 873 A.D., is believed to be hidden and is expected to appear again as Mehdi (his surname). Several Musalmans have indeed already given themselves out as this personage, and some have secured a number of followers.

The Imams are regarded by the Shiahs with intense respect and several sects believe that Ali was an incarnation. The title *Imam* means 'leader,' but it is given by Shiahs only to the twelve immediate descendants of the Prophet. The Sunnis give the title to the four learned doctors Shāfi, Hanīfa, Mālik, and Haubal, the founders of their faith, and they hold that there must be a visible Imam, or Father of the Church. The *Pesh Imam* is the leader of devotions in a Sunni mosque.

These differences have resulted in a separation between the two parties as great as that which existed in former days between the churches of Christendom; the members of each regard the others as heretics, and disputes between the two factions have been of frequent occurrence.

Outside India the Sunnis are chiefly found in Arabia, Egypt, Syria, and Turkey, and the stronghold of the Shiahs is Persia.

The Wahabis, of whom a considerable number exist in India, are followers of the doctrines of Muhammad, son of Wahab, who, in the seventeenth century, started a purifying movement against the traditions which had arisen regarding Islam and attempted to abolish the invocation of saints and spirits of the dead. He taught that shrines, *tazias*, minarets, and such like structures are an abomination; that *pirs* (religious instructors), *walis*, and saints have no spiritual powers or authority; and that tomb-worship is not only useless but repugnant. The Wahabis believe in the absolute unity of God and declare that others have perverted this faith. At one time they became powerful in Arabia and, obtaining possession of Mecca and Medina, destroyed some of the relics which were venerated there.

The Sufis (so named from *Suf*, *i.e.*, wool, as the members of this sect wore woollen garments), profess to follow the teachings of the Qoran; their doctrines are indeed a form of mysticism which may be likened to the Hindu Vedanta philosophy, although said by them to be based on the Qoran.

They are fatalists, and believe that human beings will pass through the four stages *Sharīat* (according to rule), *Tarīqat* (following the right path), *Haqīqat* (realization of the truth), and *Mārifat* (knowledge of the Divinity), and that they will finally obtain union with God; religions have no significance and there is no real difference between right and wrong; God rules everything and man is irresponsible for his actions.

They are mostly to be found in Persia and are not numerous in India. The ascetic of the Sufis is known as a *darvesh* in Turkey, Egypt, Arabia, and Persia, and in India he is classed among *fakirs*.

The Babis are a sect started in Persia during the early part of the nineteenth century by a young enthusiast named Ali, of Shiraz. He called himself the *Bab*, or 'Door,' through which God can alone be approached; he recognized Moses, Jesus, and Muhammad as the principal other Babs, declaring that there were more to come. Ali preached the unity of God and the final absorption of all things in Him and inveighed against the *pardah* system, divorce, and polygamy.

The Babs incurred the displeasure of the Persian Government and many of them, including their leader, were put to death. In 1852 some of their members attempted to assassinate the Shah, and this resulted in the general slaughter of all who were known to profess their belief. Babis can now only follow their doctrines secretly in Persia. Their bible is called the *Beyan*, and it teaches that the divine will become incarnate in the Babs. The sect is only encountered here and there in India.

The Senusi order has a large number of adherents, principally in Africa. This sect works against Western civilization and attempts to keep Islam free of all modern taint.

Ahmadis. The members of this sect are followers of Mirza Ghulam Ahmed, who resided at Kadian in the Gurdaspur district during the latter part of the nineteenth century. They regard him as a prophet second only to Muhammad. Ahmadis have their own mosques and observe the great Muslim fasts and festivals, but do not visit shrines, such as those of Baba Farid or Sakhi Sarwar, nor do they follow other Muslims at prayers. They hold a *jalsa* at Kadian during the Christmas holidays, this time having been chosen because there are general holidays then.

Saints and Superstitions.

In addition to angels and devils the Qoran teaches Muslims to believe in the existence of *genii* or *jins*; these are something more than spirits, for they propagate their species, eat, drink, and die like human beings; some are good and others evil; some are invisible and others are beings such as *peri* (fairies) and *div* (giants). They apparently have minds capable of receiving impressions, for Muhammad was sent for their conversion as well as for that of man.

At many places in the Punjab are tombs said to contain the remains of *nau-gajas* (nine-yarders), or giants, who came from Arabia in days gone by. On a large mound at Harappa in the Montgomery district there is one of these tombs which is about twenty-seven feet in length. The legend regarding it is that a giant of that height, named "Nur Shah," came into the district laying waste the countryside; the people of Harappa, however, met him with bows and arrows and attacked him so severely that he fell on the mound mortally wounded; he was buried where he fell, for the corpse was too large and heavy to remove. In proof of this story the residents point to the grave and also to certain large and peculiar stones at the foot of the mound. One of these is a black stone, about the size and shape of a millstone without a hole, which weighs over a hundredweight and is said to have formed the signet of his ring. Two others are of a curious yellow colour and of remarkable shape, being something like large knuckle bones, only more circular, and having a hole through the middle; these are almost as heavy as the signet stone and are stated to have been the giant's armlets, which fell off, together with the signet, when he stumbled. No stone of the kind is found in the Punjab, and how and why they got to Harappa is a mystery.

People carefully avoid such graves at night, for the spirits of the giants are believed to hover around and, being malignant, are likely to do them harm.

A small storeroom was once built near one of these tombs for the kitchen of a school boarding-house; during its construction one of the workmen broke his leg, and another was taken ill and died; thereafter the room remained vacant, for no one would use it.

Great respect is shown by Muslims to "saints," more especially when they are dead. Large and elaborate tombs are erected over the remains of the more celebrated ones, numbers of whom are believed to have performed miracles.

The "saint" is sometimes a *fakir*, or Muslim ascetic, who perhaps sets up as a hermit or wanders about collecting alms and food. Many of these mendicants are believed to possess the power of curing sickness, causing pregnancy in barren women, and performing miracles; most of them provide charms against disease and ill-luck. It is a common occurrence in some parts of India for a *fakir* to set up a hermitage by the grave of a deceased confrère, to pronounce him to have been a holy saint, and to collect a number of *murids* or clients; sometimes these assemblies assume large proportions, and after a time several thousand persons will attend at the annual gatherings, when each makes a cash or other offering to the custodian of the grave. As time goes on a portion of the income is spent on the construction of a masonry edifice or shrine, and a regular Fair is instituted.

A *Pir*, or religious chief man, is generally a descendant of some saint or holy person, and he is the *sajada-nashin* (occupier of the post) of the *khangah* or *makbarra* (shrine or tomb); one without heirs will appoint a successor. He sends out servants (*Pir ke Khalifa*) to collect offerings in the shape of animals, cash, and other things from his *murids* (followers) who also present gifts when visiting the shrine. Wealthy persons sometimes give land as their donations and a Musalman ruler will make a grant of land or revenue in his favour and the British Government has continued the usage in special instances, provided the buildings are maintained in proper order and the custodian continues to be of good character.

Some of the shrines are very celebrated, and many of the Pirs have an enormous number of *murids*.

In the Punjab may be mentioned the *makbarra* of Data Ganj Baksh Sahib at Lahore, the *khangah* of Baba Farid at Pakpattan, of Bahawal Haq at Multan, and of Sakhi Sarwar in the Dera Ghazi Khan district.

Near Delhi is the shrine of Kutab-ud-Din which is much visited by pilgrims and is renowned by reason of the high tower known as the "Kutab," which stands alongside.

Sayad Shah Zahur at Allahabad was a saint distinguished by his wisdom, piety, and austerity of life.

In Bombay the Agha Khan is regarded as the principal Pir of the present day, and the chief *makbarras* there are those of Mian Haji and Mai Hajani.

The name of Khwaja Moeen-ud-din Chishti of Ajmer has been revered for centuries as the chief of the Indian saints.

Below the Suleman Hills in the Dera Ghazi Khan district is the shrine of Sakhi Sarwar, known to the Hindus as *Lakhdata*, or 'Giver of Wealth' and celebrated through several centuries as the performer of wonderful miracles. He is respected by Muslims, Hindus, and Sikhs indiscriminately. Here, curiously enough, the pilgrims enter into a regular contract with the spirit of the saint; on the walls of the shrine are inscribed written promises of future payment in cash or kind if certain requests are fulfilled.

Another famous shrine is that of Baba Farid at Pakpattan. He lived some 500 years ago and was held in great esteem, both on account of his piety and the miracles he performed. It is commonly believed that he existed on a diet of stones and wooden cakes. He is known as *Shakar-*

Ganj, or 'Sugar-Store,' because anything which he put into his mouth is said to have turned into sugar. There is also a shrine to him in Ajudhan where he died in 690 H. This date is derived by Muslims from the word *makhdom* (*m*=40, *kh*=600, *d*=4, *o*=6, *m*=40). Before dying he gave out that whoever should pass through his shrine at Pakpattan on the anniversary of his death would be assured a place in paradise. During the night of the festival held annually in his honour between 50,000 and 100,000 pilgrims rush with enthusiasm to the small building which is said to contain his remains. The entrance door of the shrine is of silver and is known as the *Bihisht Darwaza* or 'Gate of Paradise.' The pilgrims consist of both Muslims and Hindus and formerly women were admitted.

It is remarkable that Hindus should so often unite with Musalmans in honouring the spirits of Muslim saints, but the fact shows how intensely the Hindu respects the souls of the departed. At Karnal in the Eastern Punjab there is a strange practice. Tradition says that a Brahman girl was abducted by a certain Raja; a saint named Asthan Sayad Mahmud led a large force of Musalmans against the tyrant and the maiden was recovered, but not before some five hundred of the rescuing warriors had lost their lives. They were honoured as *shahids* (martyrs) by the erection of small tombs at the spots where they succumbed, and every Thursday evening *fakirs* and others light little lamps at these shrines, perform certain ceremonies, and receive offerings, not from members of their own religion but from Hindus, who thus gracefully acknowledge the service rendered by the martyrs. The number of shrines, however, is now far in excess of the five hundred, for every remarkable object has been turned into one ; thus an enormous old stone which once did duty as a roller is utilized, and a *kos minar*, or milestone, forms another.

At the same place may be seen the picturesque tomb of Boali Kalandar, another celebrated saint, who is said to have resided for some time at Budha Khera, a few miles distant, and finally to have settled at Panipat. When at the former village he was visited by a famous *fakir*, who took about a ferocious tiger as a pet. They had a dispute as to which was the bigger man, and this was finally decided in the Kalandar's favour, because he produced a cow which swallowed the tiger. At Panipat he prayed so constantly that it became laborious to get water for his ablutions each time ; so he stood in the Jumna which then flowed by the town. After standing there seven years the fish had gnawed his legs and he was so stiff he could hardly move ; so he requested the river to step back seven paces. She, in her hurry to oblige the saint, went back seven *kos* and there she is to this day. He gave the Panipat people a charm which dispelled all the flies from the city ; but they grumbled and said they rather liked flies ; so he brought them back thousandfold. The people have since repented.

The Kalandar died at Budha Khera and there was a good deal of trouble about burying him. He was entombed first at Karnal; but the Panipat people claimed his body and opened the grave, upon which he sat up and looked at them until they felt ashamed. Then they took away some bricks from the grave for the foundation of a shrine; but when they opened the box at Panipat, they found his body in it. So now he has a tomb at Panipat as well as at Karnal, and not to be outdone the people at Budha Khera erected a third shrine over the wall on which he used to ride. He died in 724 Hijra.

It is not an unheard-of matter for Muslims in a Hindu village to worship the Hindu local god, and a Musalman mother, who has lost her first-born, will sometimes relapse into idolatry and make offerings to propitiate the goddess Sitala on the chance of preserving her only son from smallpox.

At Kallar Kahar in the Salt Range is a shallow lake, the water of which is salt, probably owing to the passage of springs through a seam of salt. The people of the locality, however, explain that it used to be fresh until some five hundred years ago Baba Farid of Pakpattan came that way, unknown to the villagers, and asked for a drink of water; for a joke one of the women, who were drawing water, said, "How can you drink water when it is salt?" After quenching his thirst the holy man said, "Yes, it is verily salt," and when the women next went to fetch water they found it had become salt, and so it has remained.

There is an extraordinary story about a tomb in a Musalman graveyard at Sardi, near Kallar Kahar. It is said that a particularly holy *fakir* was once taken up to heaven in a chariot from this spot, where he had resided for many years with a dog as his only companion; on the *fakir's* departure, the faithful creature was so overcome with grief that it refused to eat, drink, or move from the place, and remained there till it died. A tomb was erected over its grave, and this is regularly illuminated by Muslims as each anniversary of its death comes round. This is all the more remarkable, because the dog is usually regarded by them as an unclean animal.

The "outstretched hand" is used as an emblem or charm by Musalmans; it is called the *punjah*, and five is a favourite number with them. It is the symbol of the martyr Imam Husain and appears on the banners and poles carried at the time of Muharram.

Fakirs sometimes carry staffs surmounted with brass hands. Designs of a hand, cut out in red cloth, are stitched upon banners used by the tribesmen in their warfare on the North-West Frontier. It is said that the Prophet introduced the system of signing documents by impressing the mark of the hand upon them, but this is apparently a very ancient custom.

Precautions are nearly always taken in the manufacture of shawls, carpets, and the like, to attract the "evil eye," by leaving a small piece incomplete or by weaving in a few threads of a different colour at some point.

Musalman yokels mostly wear talismans (*tawiz*), which usually take the form of a small silver ornament or locket worn suspended from the neck or tied to the upper part of the arm; inside these are folded pieces of paper bearing extracts from the Qoran. Texts from the holy book are also inscribed upon pieces of wood and hung on string across the entrance of houses or cattle-pens during epidemics among man or beast; these charms are also suspended from the necks of valuable animals to preserve them from misfortune.

CHAPTER XIX.

Mazdeism or Zoroastrianism.

Mazdeism is the religion of the Parsees and is so called from the name of its supreme deity, but it is more popularly known perhaps as "Zoroastrianism," from the Greek rendering of its reputed founder Zertusht.

Among the Aryans who remained in Persia, religion developed on different lines to what it did with their connections in India; their belief in a supreme god, whom they called *Ahura Mazda*, the 'god of heaven,' and in *Mithra*, the 'god ofheavenly light,' was retained; they continued to worship the elements Fire, Water, and the Earth, and also respected a number of storm-myths ;. they venerated the cow and worshipped *Homa* (the liquor otherwise known as Soma). They acquired a new conception of the world and believed that its existence was limited to twelve thousand years in four periods; they learned to consider that life consists of "good thought" (*Ahura Mazda*) and "evil thought" (*Ahriman*); they had faith in the resurrection of the dead, and they disposed of corpses by exposing them to dogs and birds of prey, instead of by burning or burying.

In the eleventh or fourteenth century before Christ, while the Aryans were still dwelling in

Bactria, one of their priests, named Zertusht (Zoroaster), reformed their religion on the lines described above; and he composed songs, which formed the basis of the ancient Persian scriptures known as the *Zend-Avesta.* Unfortunately only a few of the books now remain, owing originally to the ravages of the forces under Alexander the Great, and later to action by the Muslims.

The priests of this ancient religion were the *Magi,* or 'Wise men of the East,' so often referred to in the Bible, and they were renowned as astrologers, magicians, and interpreters of dreams.

In the beginning of the eighth century A.D. a number of the Zoroastrians (or Parsees, as they are now termed, from Pars or Fars, the name of Persia) left Persia owing to persecution and settled at Sanjan, about sixty miles north of Bombay; they brought with them their scriptures and the sacred fire, re-established their religion in India, and afterwards spread all over the country, maintaining Bombay as their headquarters.

What remains of the Zend-Avesta may be divided into two portions, the *Avesta* and the *Khorda* (little) *Avesta.* The former contains the *Vandidad,* a code of religious tales and legends; the *Visparad,* a collection of sacrificial rules; the *Yasna,* a composition of litanies and old hymns. The other portion consists of a number of short prayers, which are recited both by priests and laymen at special times; they are :—the five *Gah,* the thirty formulæ of *Sirozah*, the three *Afrigan*, the six *Nyayis*, and the *Yast* or psalms.

The Parsee of to-day regards Fire as the symbol of God, much as the Christian looks to the Cross as the emblem of Christ; and it is requisite for them to turn the face towards anything that is glorious, such as the sun, the sea, or fire, when they are saying their prayers. A pious Parsee would not abuse fire, nor use it in contemptuous manner, and it follows that he does not smoke. As in ancient days, the cow is regarded as sacred; its flesh is not eaten, and *nirang*, its urine, is regarded as hallowed—to be used by the priests upon special occasions and before washing; the liquid is actually drunk by some of the orthodox during the observance of certain ceremonies, but the reforming Parsee objects to its use.

The only offering now made at the temples is the libation of the sacred juice *Homa*, which is regarded as particularly divine.

The Parsees believe in a paradise called *Gurasman Bihisht*, where the souls of the good go after crossing a bridge known as *Chinvad*, and they have a hell termed *Dozakh*, a dark place with fiends, where Ahriman (Shaitan or Satan) dwells as the arch-fiend.

There are a number of angels, who are occasionally invoked, such as Sravsha the guardian of the souls of the dead, Spenta Armati guardian of the earth, and Hom who is addressed as the destroyer of all that is wicked.

The modern Parsees, however, maintain that, according to the original teaching of Zoroaster, prayer to spirits other than the Supreme God is not correct, and their creed may be summarized as follows :—

To know God as the one Supreme Being.

To recognize Zoroaster as his inspired prophet.

To believe the religion of the Avesta, as brought by him from God, as entirely true.

To perform good deeds and trust in the goodness of God.

To be moral in thought, word, and deed.

To shun evil and wickedness.

To pray five times a day.

To believe in divine judgment on the fourth day after death.

To hope for heaven and fear hell.

To believe in a general resurrection.

To turn towards some luminous object while worshipping God.

Ahura Mazda (Ormuzd) is the creator of all things ; he has done what he willed and shall do what he wills ; he alone can save.

The priests consist of the *Dasturs* or high priests, the *Mobeds* or middle order, and the *Herbads* or lower order ; they are hereditary but their sons may become laymen. Dasturs are the authorities on all religious matters, and they impose penalties and decide questions relating to doctrine. There was, for some time, a council or *panchayat*, consisting of six Dasturs and twelve Mobeds, which settled the affairs of the community generally, but their powers were restricted in relation to marriage and divorce by Act XV of 1865, and in respect to questions of succession by Act XXI of the same year ; the functions of the council or committee now consist chiefly in its being trustee to certain charitable funds.

The priests officiate at the fire-temples of which there are two classes, namely, the seven *Atash-Bahrams* and a large number of *Atash-Adarans*. They maintain a continual watch over the sacred fire, so that it never goes out, and they feed it with sandal-wood and gum benzoin. It is kept in a large urn on a stone altar, which is situate in a shrine within an outer court of the temple where its light can be seen by the worshippers. The priest sits crossed-legged within the shrine facing the fire and holding the *baresma*, or the sacrificial besom made of silver rods, in his left hand.

Devotions at the fire-altars are performed by the laity of both sexes, but they are optional and may be carried out at any time by the worshippers, who usually contribute something to the priests. The pious Parsee, however, will say prayers many times a day—on rising in the morning, after ablutions and meals, and before retiring to rest.

The Parsee infant must be born upon the ground-floor, and its mother should not be seen by the family for forty days. On the seventh day an astrologer-priest is called in, and he announces a number of auspicious names from which the parents make a selection.

At the age of six years and three months the child is received into the Zoroastrian religion by a rite of initiation, which consists of washing with *nirang* and investiture with the *kusti*, or sacred cord, and with the *sudra*, or sacred shirt.

The *kusti* is a thin woollen cord of 72 threads (to represent the 72 *has*, or chapters, of the Yasna); it has two small tails at each end to denote the four seasons and three knots on each tail for the twelve months of the year. The *sudra* is made of cotton cloth, gauze, or net. Both boys and girls are invested with these articles, and before initiation they wear a *jubhla* or silk frock. A priest ties a cord round the waist of the child, upon whom he pronounces a blessing and then throws sliced fruit, seeds, perfumes, and spices over its head. If a child dies before initiation it is considered as returned to Ahura Mazda, pure as upon entry into the world; for children are not regarded as accountable for their actions until within their seventh year. It is the *kusti* to which Moore alludes in his "Lalla Rookh," when he makes Hafiz thus declare himself a fire-worshipper :—

"Hold! hold! thy words are death,
The stranger cried, as wide he flung
His mantle back, and show'd beneath
The Gebi belt that round him hung."

The Persian word "*gabr*" signifies a fire worshipper or any unbeliever in Islam.

A Parsee may only have one wife at a time.

The day for a marriage is fixed by an astrologer who consults the stars for the purpose. Invitations for the ceremony are issued through the priest. Shortly before sunset the wedding procession sets out with music and pomp from the house of the bridegroom for that of the bride's father, where a reception takes place and the presents, sent beforehand, are displayed. Ladies escort the bridegroom into the bride's house, and his future mother-in-law meets him at the entrance, throwing fruit and rice at his feet. The fathers sit down side by side and between them stands the priest. The happy couple then sit on chairs opposite one another and are linked together by a silken cord, which is wound round them as the ceremony proceeds, the bride being under a veil of silk or muslin. The priest burns incense and repeats a nuptial benediction in Zend and Sanskrit; after which the bride and bridegroom throw rice over one another, and the priest scatters some on their heads in token of a wish for abundance. Bouquets are now handed to the guests and otto of roses is sprinkled over them; the newly married couple then eat sweetmeats and thereafter the guests do the same.

A procession is formed and the bridegroom is conducted with music and lanterns to his own house where there is a feast until midnight, when the guests return to the residence of the bride, whom they escort and hand over to the bridegroom. Eight days later a wedding feast of vegetables and wine is provided by the newly married pair and toasts are then proposed.

When a Parsee is dying, a priest attends and reads portions of the Avesta, consisting of consoling texts and prayers for forgiveness ; he also administers the sacred cup of Homa. Directly death occurs the body is taken to the ground-floor where it is laid on the floor, washed, dressed in white, perfumed, and placed on an iron trestle. The rite of *sag-did* (dog-gaze) is performed before the removal of the corpse ; this consists of bringing a dog to look at the body ; some say that this practice is for ascertaining the state of the departed soul by the action of the animal; others that its view will expedite the translation of the soul to heaven. The priest offers prayers for the repose of the soul, and male friends call, make obeisance at the door and express their regrets.

A corpse is regarded as unclean, so everything which it touches must be destroyed or purified, and the bier is carried by four pall-bearers, who in Bombay belong to a class of Parsees called *Nessus* (unclean) *salar*. The funeral procession is headed by priests and proceeds to the *Dokhma* (Tower of Silence) where, after prayer, the body is exposed on an iron grating to be devoured by vultures and birds of prey ; the bones are afterwards allowed to crumble away. Parsees do not inter or burn their dead, for it is considered that the earth and fire would be contaminated thereby.

On the third day after death friends and relations collect at the residence of the deceased and proceed thence to a fire-temple (*sagri*) where prayers are offered and a list of charities is handed over to the priest. Payments are also made for monthly prayers for the soul of the deceased during a period of one year and thereafter on each anniversary of the death.

In Bombay the " Towers of Silence " are situate in a beautiful garden on Malabar Hill.

Chapters XI, XII, XV, and XVIII of Leviticus describe very nearly some of the customs of the Parsees, if we omit those portions relating to sacrifices, circumcision, uncleanness until even three score and ten days for purification after birth of a daughter.

Their sacred books do not degrade women, and although formerly there was a certain amount of *pardah*, Parsee ladies of to-day are free to move in society and, what is more, set a very good example by their modesty and chastity.

The Parsees generally are an exceptionally cleanly and benevolent race, and a Parsee beggar is unknown.

Calendar. There are twelve months of thirty days each in the Parsee year and five days, or *Gatha*, are added to make up the deficiency.

The names of the months are :—

1. Farvardin.	4. Tir.
2. Ardibehisht.	5. Amardad.
3. Khurdad.	6. Sharivar.

7. Meher.
8. Aban.
9. Adar.
10. Deh.
11. Bahman.
12. Asfandar.

The days of the month are named after celestial and other beings, but the fact that the 1st Ormazd, the 8th Dep-Adar, the 15th Dep-Meher, and the 23rd Dep-Din are sacred to Ormazd, affords evidence of a Sunday and of an older division into weeks.

About the beginning of the eighteenth century it was discovered that the date of the calendar then used in India differed from that in use by their brethren in Persia, and the discussion, which thereupon arose as to which was correct, led to the formation of two sects among the Parsees. Those who adopted the newly imported date of Persia call themselves the *Kadimi* (ancient), or *Churigarian*, and begin their year a month earlier; those who continued the Indian date are known as the *Rasami* (customary), or *Shahanshahi* (of the King of Kings), and are the more numerous. In respect to all other matters the two parties are in agreement.

A special feature of the Parsee calendar is the importance placed upon special days for particular acts; thus the first day of a month is auspicious for entering a new house and others are best for setting out upon a journey or for starting a new business and so on.

Their day is divided into watches (*gah*), four in winter and five in summer; each *gah* has a heavenly watcher and its own special prayers.

The Zoroastrian theory of Creation is that the world was created in 365 days divided into six unequal periods; these periods are marked by six *Gahambar*, or days of rest, and on these occasions, in accordance with a good old custom, the Parsees—high and low, rich and poor—partake of food together and unite in prayer.

Festivals. Parsee festivals are numerous, but they are celebrated with none of the noise and merriment of the Hindu fairs; there are no evil spirits to be appeased, no cruel goddesses to be propitiated; and the religious ceremonies are conducted without pomp and with little show.

The 1st of Farvardin is the "New Year's Day" of the Parsees, who call it *Pateti*; on that day they pay honour to Yezdejird, the last king of the Sassanian dynasty, for their calendar is founded on his era and Zoroastrianism was the State religion of the Sassanian period. Formerly this was a great day for special worship at the fire-temples, but its observance is perhaps more social nowadays than religious. On this day the people rise early and, after prayers and ablutions, put on new clothes, worship at the temples, and afterwards exchange visits with their friends, offering them good wishes and joining hands; alms are given to the poor and servants are provided with new uniforms.

Khordad-sal is another important festival; it is held on the 6th Farvardin in memory of Zoroaster, who is believed to have been born in North Persia on that day.

Amardad-sal, held on the following day, is in honour of Amardad, the angel of immortality.

Ava Ardu Sur Jasan is the festival of Ava, the angel presiding over the sea. Parsees go to the seashore or a river-bank, chant prayers, and offer flowers, sugar, and cocoanuts—customs which they have borrowed from the Hindus. In Bombay a fair is held on the Esplanade on this day.

In midwinter (*Media Spamor*) there is a feast lasting for six days in commemoration of the six days of Creation, and in the Spring occurs a festival in honour of agriculture.

Mithra, the angel directing the course of the sun, is honoured on the 16th day of Meher, when there is also a festival to celebrate truth and friendship.

On the 10th day of Aban; Farvardin, the guardian angel of souls of the departed, is respected, and this day is specially devoted to ceremonies of the dead; people attend at the Towers of Silence where prayers are offered.

The last ten days of the year should be spent in deeds of charity and thanksgiving to Ahura Mazda.

These are the principal festivals of these remarkable people, and nowadays they are regarded much in the same manner as are Saints' Days by Christians.

CHAPTER XX.

THE MANAGEMENT OF FAIRS.

PUBLISHED official reports on the conduct of fairs at the great religious centres of India in the early part of the nineteenth century reveal a shocking state of affairs.

The wretched pilgrims—men, women, and children—wended their way in thousands along the main roads towards the sacred places, crowding the villages and halting places, creating an artificial famine like a swarm of locusts, drinking infected water and eating impure food, and offering themselves as a prey to bands of marauders. Arrived at their destination these weary enthusiasts would be crammed into the most filthy hovels by way of lodging-houses—often for weeks together—in the rainy season beneath leaky roofs and on miry floors, the space allotted per head being just as much as they could cover lying down and sometimes even less. Here, with insufficient food—and bad at that—attacked by vermin and disease, thousands received relief in death. Of those who escaped from these pest-houses with their foul surroundings, many found themselves without money and had to beg their way home, but more often died of exhaustion and want of food; others fell sick and succumbed in agony, unattended and uncared for; yet others carried disease with them to their homes, where, maybe, thousands died in consequence; the return of the pilgrim streams was, indeed, the signal for the spread of epidemics throughout the country.

Steps have long since been taken by the British Government to mitigate these horrors, and with a great measure of success. It is, however, exceedingly difficult to protect the enormous masses of pilgrims in India from disease, to help them against themselves; it is by no means only the want of education which causes this lethargy, for even those who are educated seem willing to undergo risk of infection on sacred occasions by crowding into places which rapidly become insanitary and by drinking and bathing in the polluted water of holy tanks and streams.

It may prove of interest to mention briefly certain measures which are useful in dealing with a large religious *mela*.

In the first place a set of standing orders should be carefully prepared in eight parts under the following heads:—

(1) General Instructions, (2) Fair Establishment, (3) Collection of Fees, (4) Inquiry Offices and Block Officers, (5) Medical Arrangements, (6) Drinking Water-supply, (7) Conservancy, (8) Police Arrangements.

A copy of the standing order relating to his particular department should be supplied to every responsible official employed at the fair, and a set of all the orders should be in the hands of each officer on duty.

(1) *General Instructions.*—These contain directions regarding preliminary arrangements; such as the despatch of statistics and information to the railway companies concerned, so that pilgrim trains may be provided and special arrangements made at the Fair stations and at halting places *en route* (30 trains a day can be arranged on a single line so as to carry off about 60,000 in three days); the sanitation of halting places and disinfection of wells on the routes to the fair; clearing of jungle and laying out of sites for camps, spit-locking of roads; repair of bathing-ghats, embankments, drains, and wells; disinfection of water-supply; collection of material and supplies, lighting contract, construction of huts, and erection of tents for officers, officials, hospital, police, toll-posts, inquiry offices, and so on; digging of trenches and erection of screens for conservancy purposes; preparation of budget of income and expenditure, printing of rules and ticket-books; supply of tin discs for Brahmans entitled to officiate and accept offerings, and of passes for officials and others on duty.

For a fair of 500,000 Hindu pilgrims in the open the following list gives a rough idea of the miscellaneous articles required for official use:—

80 wooden cash-boxes with padlocks for use at toll-posts.

Sealing-wax, cloth, candles, and matches for sealing padlocks at the Fair office.

Pens, ink, and paper for the various offices.

Coarse grass for the thatches of the hospital huts and for placing on the steps of ghats to prevent slipping.

600 *dols*, for drawing water at the wells and 300 iron pails with ropes.

150 hurricane lanterns.

100 lamps on posts.

30 Kitson lights (on hire).

120 shuldaris for toll-posts and camp offices., etc.

25 cases of kerosine oil.

Flags. 76 white with red circle, on poles, for drinking wells.

10 white with red hand, on poles, for inquiry offices.

30 large red, on poles, for latrines.

120 small red, on bamboos, for latrines.

50 small white, for refuse trenches.

110 sacks containing 165 maunds of quicklime for disinfecting wells and other places.

1,800 *gharas* for offices and camps.

600 screens of *chatai* or *sirki* for use at latrines, each 18ft. × 4ft. with three bamboo supports.

500 baskets and brooms for sweepers.

Ropes, bamboos, and iron pegs for the *ghats*.

Wooden frames with wheels for drawing water at the wells.

500 small brass bowls for use at drinking wells.

500 earthenware pots for marking camps, etc.

Tent-pegs, firewood, and grass, etc., for officers' camp.

Charpoys, cooking-utensils, and ten *doolis* for the hospitals.

Engineering tools, such as hoes, spades, pick-axes, etc.

Many yards of muslin for compulsory sale to the keepers of food-shops.

Boats and rafts, posts and ropes, water-cisterns and railway sleepers.

Whenever possible it is desirable to prevent pilgrims from entering a town, and, where this cannot be done for religious reasons, there must be strict rules to prevent overcrowding in lodging-houses, while the intramural conservancy, drainage, and water-supply must be thorough.

Shops for supply of provisions and fruit, vegetables and cooked food, require careful supervision and excise shops more than ordinary control. It is most necessary to induce the local Brahmans and others to erect temporary sheds of a suitable nature in the camp marked out beforehand, and much can be done by establishing a good bazar in a central position in the camp.

(2) *Fair Establishment.*—A list should be prepared of the establishment required, with columns to show where they are to be supplied from, and a second list should show their distribution on arrival.

For a *mela* of this size some 500 *kahars*, 100 *bhistis* with *mashaks*, 500 sweepers, 60 sweepresses, 50 labourers, 400 to 500 *chowkidars* (village watchmen), 100 *patwaris* (village accountants), 100 *lambardars* (headmen), with a large number of clerks, members of local bodies, and several officers are required, exclusive of the police and medical establishments.

Each officer in charge of the various departments—such as conservancy, water-supply, and so on—receives his allotted staff from the Fair manager as it arrives and sets to work in accordance with his standing order. Every one knows what his duty is, and it remains for the supervising officers merely to see that the orders are obeyed.

(3) *Collection of Fees.*—Fees may be arranged for collection at the following rates :—

		Rs.	A.		Rs.	A.
1. Each pilgrim (including children) ..	..	0	1			
2. Each shop ..	from	1	0	to	5	0
Hawkers ..	„	0	8	to	1	0
Petty shops having a frontage of less than 6 feet, if the owners are poor or doing a small business	from	0	4	to	0	8
3. Each draft or riding animal and each goat, sheep, buffalo, or cow	..	0	1			
4. Each vehicle ..	..	0	4			
5. Each vehicle plying for hire in the Fair area	..	2	0			
6. Admission tickets to the town per person (where the fair is outside) ..	..	3	0			

7. Rent of land (belonging to a local body or temporarily acquired) at 6 pies per square foot within central limits and at 3 pies per square foot elsewhere.

Tickets of different colours are required for each of the above; other free tickets should be issued to the townspeople according to the latest census numbers and tickets of a separate colour are required for bonâ fide *sadhus*.

The fees are collected and tickets issued when pilgrims enter the Fair area at the toll-posts, each of which must have an establishment of say 2 to 5 *patwaris*, 2 *lambardars*, 1 *zaildar*, 1 or 2 *chuprassis*, 4 to 12 *chowkidars*, 1 head constable, and 2 to 6 constables; the assessment of shops, of vehicles plying for hire, and of rent can be carried out by small committees working under members of the local board.

(4) *Inquiry Offices and Block Officers.*—The camp for pilgrims is divided into blocks, each of which is in charge of a block officer, who has at his head-quarters an inquiry office. He has an establishment under him. His duties consist of making himself acquainted with the orders issued, communicating them to the public, supervising everything within his block, and assisting the pilgrims in every manner possible. Should a lost child be found, or a parent searching for such, they are at once sent to the central police station; sick people are conducted to the general hospital; should a dispute occur the block officer must, if possible,

decide it; if a pilgrim wishes to know the time of a train he must be informed; when trespassers on the roads are found he must remove them.

(5) *Medical Arrangements.*—These consist of fully equipped general, police, and isolation hospitals and an ambulance detachment. A number of vaccinators are attached to the blocks for first-aid and other duties, a special staff is on duty at the railway station and at toll-posts for detection of disease among incoming pilgrims. Special duties are assigned to the medical establishment during bathing ceremonies and for inspection of food in the bazar, of the drinking water and sanitation generally.

(6) *Drinking Water-supply.*—Where drinking water has to be obtained from wells, elaborate arrangements have to be made to protect it. Those wells which are unfit for use must be effectually closed; special persons are appointed to draw the water and no unauthorized vessel must be let into a well. Large galvanized iron cisterns, provided with taps and protected by thatch, are useful at the much frequented wells. Every well must be disinfected before the fair commences.

(7) *Conservancy.*—The most suitable method is the trench and screen system. Gangs of labourers should be continually employed to dig the trenches one foot deep, one foot wide, and one foot apart. These are gradually covered with loose earth as they are used. In case of heavy rain filling the trenches the earth must be put in as soon as possible.

(8) *Police Arrangements.*—The force required for duty at the fair, exclusive of railway police, may consist of 1 Superintendent, 1 Deputy Superintendent, 4 European Inspectors or Sergeants, 4 Inspectors, 25 Sub-Inspectors, 55 Head Constables, 500 Constables, 12 Mounted Constables, and 40 Detectives.

In addition to their ordinary duties of watch and ward, investigation of crime, and arrest of offenders, the police at a fair have heavy duties to perform in controlling the crowds during the bathing or other ceremonies and on the occasion of arrival and departure of trains; they have also to control the traffic on the main roads and assist when necessary in first-aid.

At places, such as a railway station, where there is likely to be a rush by thousands of pilgrims at the close of a fair, it is necessary to provide in the yard a long row of pens (each with food, drinking-water, and conservancy arrangements); outside these should be the ticket office sheds, and the outer wall of the station yard should be about eight feet high; projecting outwards at right angles from the outer wall, and opposite each booking office, there should be a passage consisting of two *kacha* walls, ninety feet long, two feet apart, two feet thick, and seven feet high. The largest crowd can be effectually controlled by means of such a passage which only admits persons in single file. When a rush occurs the people shoot past on either side of the entrance and then have to circle round in order to make another attempt to enter. They soon get tired of doing so and gradually become content to sit down quietly at a distance in rows, when they can be arranged in small parties and each sent through in single file. Directly there is a sufficient number round a booking office inside the station yard, a signal is given and the nearest passage is closed by one or two constables standing inside the entrance to the passage.

Parties of rural notables should be told off to assist the pilgrims in getting their tickets and to see that they are not swindled.

Women and children, cripples and old men should be escorted through the passage after selection from the waiting crowd.

It is important that a large number of pens should be used for each train and that each pen should only have in it a number small enough for easy control. The pens should be opened one at a time when a train has to be loaded, and then again it is the weak who require assistance and protection.

A gateway or any kind of opening in a straight wall, when unprovided with a projecting passage, is a trap towards which the crowd concentrates and where crushing cannot fail to occur.

Palings of wooden railway sleepers, stuck vertically with two feet of their ends in the ground make very effectual barriers and when successive rows are placed at a slant *en échelon* are most useful for dividing up a crowd advancing, say, on the dangerous part of a tank.

It is most necessary for an officer controlling a large sacred fair to have a thorough knowledge of the religious customs and ceremonies to be observed, and to work out beforehand the most suitable arrangements for enabling the pilgrims to properly perform their religious duties. Such knowledge will facilitate matters when a dispute has to be decided, will enable the officer to have a sympathy with the people which he could hardly possess otherwise, and will tend to mitigate the hardships which thousands of earnest Indians have to endure in the observance of their religious beliefs.

INDEX.

The following list forms both a glossary and index.